How to use
INTEREST RATE FUTURES CONTRACTS

How to use
INTEREST RATE FUTURES
CONTRACTS

Edward W. Schwarz

DOW JONES-IRWIN
Homewood, Illinois 60430

ISBN 0-87094-180-1
Library of Congress Catalog Card No. 79-51781

Printed in the United States of America

1 2 3 4 5 6 7 8 9 0 K 6 5 4 3 2 1 0 9

I dedicate this book to my wife,
Shirlee,
whose constant support and inspiration
was the catalyst of this endeavor.

Foreword

Prior to October 1975 there was no such thing as an interest rate or financial instrument futures contract. During that month the Chicago Board of Trade introduced futures trading in GNMA certificates. The Board of Trade was relying on the acceptance of a very basic premise when it launched this new contract. This premise is that money—or more precisely the cost of money—can be viewed the same as any other commodity. In fact, it is really no different than soybeans or silver in its "commodity fundamentals." For instance, the *price* of money varies considerably; its price varies according to the laws of *supply* and *demand;* it has a very high degree of *fungibility*; and the *risks* inherent in handling money are such that many types of businesses would like to pass those risks on to others via an appropriate *hedging* mechanism.

This premise that the cost of money is a commodity has quickly gained widespread acceptance. In only four years a rather large family of financial instrument futures contracts has emerged. A look at those contracts already established as well as those being proposed will attest to the dynamic growth in this area.

Established contracts

CDR GNMA
CD GNMA
Treasury bonds
90-day commercial paper
Three-month Treasury bill
One-year Treasury bill
30-day commercial paper
Treasury notes (4-6 year)

Proposed contracts

Eurodollar certificate of
  deposit
Dow Jones average

Another indication of the tremendous potential for financial instrument futures is that almost *every* commodity and security exchange in the United States, as well as some abroad, either is already offering financial instrument futures or will soon be doing so.

It is interesting to compare the short history of financial futures with that of commodity futures trading in general. The first financial entry, GNMA futures, has already established itself as perhaps the most successful commodity futures contract ever initiated. The next two contracts introduced, three-month Treasury bills and long-term U.S. Treasury bonds, are progressing equally well. Given the large number of contracts introduced or proposed to date, the question must be asked as to where this exciting new futures family will be in five to ten years.

One conventional method of estimating future growth in commodity futures trading is to look at the underlying "cash" or "actual" commodity. For example, soybeans (the perennial volume leader in futures trading) have an annual cash crop valued at approximately $11 billion. If one were to compare the cash "crop" size of such commodities as GNMAs, U.S. Treasury bills, U.S. government bonds, U.S. government notes, commercial paper, Eurodollar CDs, and others with the corresponding figures for the grain, meal, and metal complexes, the conclusion is very impressive. It is possible that trading in financial instrument futures *could* be of greater magnitude than the combined trading total of all other commodities that are traded today!

Therefore, Mr. Schwarz's book comes at a very appropriate time. Financial instrument futures are still in an embryonic stage and this book should serve as a most welcome primer.

July 1979   ***Ronald F. Young***
                                                          Past Chairman,
                                                          Chicago Board of Trade

Preface

This book is a primer of the fundamentals of commodity trading and the concepts of interest rate futures contracts. I have provided scores of practical examples of how to use all the interest rate futures contracts. My purpose in writing this book is to provide sufficient information for professional traders, financial executives, and investors, so that they can successfully meet their financial objectives.

This primer evolved from my work on the Mortgage Bankers Committee to study all the aspects of trading mortgage securities on the Chicago Board of Trade (CBOT). When I joined the committee I was certain that trading financial instruments as commodity contracts would be neither beneficial nor practical. I changed my mind. These contracts can provide protection from interest rate movements. Even after this was proven over a one-year trading period, very few money managers, treasurers, or knowledgeable investors were participating in this market.

The CBOT asked me to assist in publicizing this market and to educate and advise the financial community on its advantages.

This book began with those endeavors and is the result of my contacts with hundreds of money market participants and several government agencies.

For those readers who may want more background on the entire money market, I recommend Marcia Stigum's *The Money Market: Myth, Reality and Practice* (1978). For those who may want more background on commodity trading, there are several good books to read, one of which is Bruce G. Gould's *Dow Jones-Irwin Trading Guide to Commodities Trading* (1973).

I wish to express my appreciation to the following individuals who took time to read, criticize, and encourage my efforts: Harry H. Appel; Lloyd Besant; Willian H. Bohnsack; Robert E. Burmeister; Thomas C. Coleman; Robert C. Collet; James J. Connolly; and Ronald J. Frost. Also to John Harding; Paul D. Johns; Phillip E. Kidd; Warren W. Lebeck; James M. Kinney; Alfred J. Patti; Kenneth M. Plant; Leslie Rosenthal; Richard L. Sandor; Alex Schneiderman; Louis M. Skydell; Kenneth J. Thygerson; and Ronald F. Young.

July 1979   *Edward W. Schwarz*

Contents

Chapter 1

Commodity trading: An introduction

In the mid-1840s Chicago was becoming an agricultural market-place. The last of the Indian Wars in the area ended in 1832, and settlers were coming to farm what would become the best lands in the world for growing grains. The Illinois-Michigan Canal was being completed to make transportation to and from the East simpler and cheaper. A harbor was being built in Chicago to facilitate lake and river shipping. Telegraph lines reached the city in 1848, bringing orders for agricultural products from the East and Europe. In short, communications and transportation systems were helping to make Chicago a major market.

By 1848 Chicago was the market center for products from the farmlands of Illinois, Michigan, Indiana, and Wisconsin. Marketing, however, was erratic and seasonal. In the fall, large quantities of grain came to Chicago in loaded carts that sometimes stretched for miles. Grain was cheap in the fall and then expensive in the spring when supplies were depleted. The price of bread could triple, or increase even more, between October and February. There were few storage facilities in Chicago to alleviate this feast-to-famine cycle. There was a need for an organized market to attract capital for developing storage facilities and to insure a dependable grain supply.

In 1848, 82 merchants formed the Board of Trade of the City of Chicago,

> to maintain a commercial exchange; to promote uniformity in the cus-
> toms and usages of merchants; to inculcate principles of justice and
> equity to trade; to facilitate the speedy adjustments of disputes; to
> acquire and disseminate valuable commercial and economic informa-
> tion; and generally to secure to its members the benefits of cooperation
> in the furtherance of the legitimate pursuits.

With the availability of an organized marketplace, individuals with capital invested in storage facilities. The Board of Trade itself used the aggregate political influence of its membership to work toward improving transportation and to create laws that would facilitate trade. Order began to replace chaos. Surplus grain, which earlier would have been dumped in the fall rather than returned unsold to farms, was stored in available space. Merchants and speculators were willing to bear the cost of storing grain because they knew it would be needed later and orders would be forthcoming.

A particular trading practice developed during this early period and was used both inside and outside the exchange. This was *forward contracting,* whereby a producer would agree to sell grain to a buyer at some time after the harvest. In times of heavy surplus or shortage, and corresponding very low or very high prices, default by either the buyer or seller was common. This was referred to as a *soft contract.* To resolve this problem, the practice developed of both buyer and seller depositing money with a third party as a performance bond. This eventually evolved into the concept of margin money deposited as performance bonds by all buyers and sellers of future contracts. These were recorded by clerks of the various trading firms, and later by a department of the exchange known as the clearinghouse. Much later, in 1925, an independent organization, the Clearing Corporation of the Board of Trade of the City of Chicago, was formed to function as the third-party guarantor for all futures transactions. The Chicago Mercantile Exchange formed in 1919 also established an independent clearinghouse to perform clearing operations.

As trading volume increased, the mechanisms of delivery had to change. Initially, a contract was traded through a chain of buyers and sellers, and the last buyer took delivery from the first seller. To simplify the delivery process, a third-party practice developed. Each buy and sell transaction was recorded in the exchange's clearing process. At the time of delivery, the clearing office issued warehouse receipts,[1] which were used to document delivery by the sellers, to the outstanding buyers. In addition to simplifying the delivery process, this clearing mechanism facilitated easy interchangeability and offset of futures contracts. A sale of a contract could be offset easily by buying a contract for the same delivery month. A trader's position then became net zero with the exchange's clearing office. This offset capability allowed people to trade who did not want to make or take delivery of the actual commodity. It attracted an increasing amount of speculative venture capital to the marketplace and created the market liquidity necessary for increasing the use of futures markets by hedgers.[2] Today almost all trades are settled by offset.

By the early 1870s, the elements of a futures market were in place:

1. A standard quantity with quality determined by inspection and grading.
2. Payment of premiums or discounts in price for grain of greater or lesser than standard quality.
3. Payment by buyers and sellers of performance bonds held by a third party.
4. Established future delivery dates.
5. The interchangeability of futures contracts of the same delivery month and the ability to offset.
6. Prices negotiated by open outcry in the marketplace.

Between 1870 and 1920 exchange self regulation gave way to a demand for government controls. Congress passed the Futures Trading Act of 1921, but the act was later declared unconstitutional on an issue of taxing power under the U.S. Constitution. This legislation was reintroduced in 1922 as the Grain Futures Act. It was then based on the interstate commerce clause of the

---

[1] A warehouse receipt is a document guaranteeing the existence and availability of a given quantity and quality of a commodity in a precise storage location. It is used as a transfer of ownership in both cash and selected futures contracts.

[2] See Chapter 3.

Constitution and was passed by the Congress and upheld in the courts. This legislation remained in force until 1936, when it was amended and coverage was extended to cotton and other specified commodities. This resulted in the Commodity Exchange Act of 1936. An important change in the legislation was the creation of the Commodity Exchange Authority, operating under the Secretary of Agriculture, as the official regulatory agency. A new aspect of this legislation was the requirement that brokerage firms segregate all margin monies[3] received on deposit against futures positions from working funds of the firm and from margins on securities accounts. The legislation further enforced the principle that the exchanges are responsible for regulating their own members and member firms under their rules and regulations. Further amendments to the Commodity Exchange Act of 1936 were made in 1968, emphasizing the responsibilities of all exchanges to regulate themselves.

There was a new wave of agitation for more uniform regulation of futures markets in the early 1970s. In 1974 Congress passed the Commodity Futures Trading Commission Act, which became effective in April 1975. Its major significance was the extension of regulation to all futures trading in all commodities, not just to the traditional agricultural futures markets.

A second major significance of the act of 1974 was that it was the enabling legislation for a new independent U.S. agency, the Commodity Futures Trading Commission, which was charged with the regulation of all U.S. futures markets. The commission, consisting of five commissioners appointed by the President and subject to approval by the U.S. Senate, operates with a staff that is now fully independent of the U.S. Department of Agriculture.

THE DEVELOPMENT OF HEDGING

As the experience with futures trading developed, market participants began to note a fundamental aspect of price movement that still constitutes the basic premise of hedging. Cash prices and

---

[3] See Chapter 3

futures prices tend to move in the same direction as they respond to underlying conditions of supply and demand. When it is thought that supplies are relatively scarce compared with demand, prospective sellers naturally tend to raise their offering prices. This is true of both sellers of the actual commodity and sellers of futures contracts for the commodity. Conversely, when it is thought that supplies are relatively large compared with demand, prospective buyers of both the actual commodity and the futures contracts for the commodity tend to lower their bids. Cash and futures prices thus naturally tend to rise and fall in roughly parallel movement as they respond individually to an underlying common set of supply and demand factors. Once this aspect of price movement was noted by market participants, they realized that action could be taken in futures contracts to minimize their risks of financial loss due to sharply rising or falling prices. This action came to be known as *hedging.*

The grain farmer risks receiving a price for grain that does not cover the cost of production, or return a profit. The farmer has learned that risk can be minimized by selling the appropriate grain futures contracts in an amount that approximates the expected production of grain. If, as feared, the supplies at harvest time are very large and prices are low, the farmer receives less for the sale of the actual crop. However, because the farmer sold the grain futures contracts at an earlier higher price, he or she can now buy back a similar number of grain futures contracts at a lower price. This transaction earns an amount that approximates the reduced income from selling the actual commodity.

The hedge and its results are illustrated on the next page:

This example is highly simplified; the loss on the cash sale of wheat is matched exactly by earnings on futures contracts. This rarely happens, however. Usually cash and futures prices tend to move in parallel fashion but rarely by equal amounts. This is an example of a *short*, or selling, hedge. Similar examples of this technique used to protect the value of financial assets will be provided in later chapters. Simply, the short hedge provides the means of controlling or minimizing the risk of financial loss due to lower prices or higher interest rates.

Cash market	Futures market

Cash market   *Futures market*

May

Expects to harvest wheat in August with price objective of $2.35 per bushel

May

Sells September wheat futures at $2.37 per bushel

August

Sells wheat at $2.28 per bushel in the cash market

August

Buys September wheat futures at $2.30 per bushel

Result

Receives 7 cents per bushel less than price

Result

Earns 7 cents per bushel on hedge

$2.28   per bushel cash income
0.07   per bushel earned on hedge
$2.35   per bushel—objective price

On the other hand, users of basic commodities, like wheat, face the opposite risk of that faced by the wheat farmer. Producers, such as the flour miller, are in business to provide a steady supply of the commodity to their customers at stable prices. Often the miller is called upon to quote selling prices for flour that will be delivered many weeks or months in the future. In such cases, the miller is unable to buy the wheat for milling until just before the flour is delivered. In the meantime, there is nothing to prevent wheat prices from rising to an extent that will either erase the miller's projected profit or produce a loss on the forward sale of flour.

These experiences taught the millers that by purchasing wheat futures contracts equal to their commitments to sell flour for future delivery, they could be protected against rising wheat prices. Suppose, as feared, that by the time the miller is ready to buy stocks of wheat for milling, the price of wheat has risen substantially. The miller then pays significantly more for the wheat needed. However, futures prices have risen proportionally, and it is now possible to sell the same number of wheat futures contracts at the current higher price. The miller's earnings on futures contracts approximately offset the increased cost incurred in buying wheat at a later date.

The action in the cash and futures markets can be illustrated as follows:

Cash market	Futures market
October	**October**
Agrees to deliver flour in January based on expected cost of $2.30 per bushel	Buys March wheat futures contracts at $2.28 per bushel
January	**January**
Buys cash wheat at $2.35 per bushel	Sells March futures contracts at $2.43¾ per bushel
Result	**Result**
Pays 5 cents higher cost for wheat	Earns 4¾ cents per bushel on hedge

$2.35   cash cost for wheat
0.04¾   earned on hedge
$2.30¼   actual cost of wheat

This, too, is a highly simplified example and is an almost perfect hedge. More often price changes in the cash market and in the futures market are not identical. Later chapters will provide further examples of how a *long,* or buying, hedge can be used in money markets to provide opportunities to maximize future investments when lower interest rates are projected.

An additional contribution of futures markets that should not be underestimated is their value as a price reference. Users of futures markets learned early that the futures price in actively traded liquid markets could be used as a reliable indicator for establishing prices on transactions in basic commodities. In the case of wheat, the futures price represents the best informed judgment of numerous buyers and sellers as to the relative supply and demand, expressed in dollars, for wheat at specified times in the future. It is used worldwide in establishing prices on export transactions.

In addition to providing a means of minimizing price risk, hedging in futures markets provides important financial benefits. One such benefit is leverage in acquiring needed capital. Producers of hedged commodities are often able to borrow as much as 85 percent of the market value of the commodity, because lenders understand that such hedged loans contain less risk than do those of unhedged crops. Warehouse managers and merchandisers of commodities, such as grain elevator companies, who hedge can obtain more easily the large amounts of capital needed to finance costly physical plants and ongoing purchases of grain. Users of basic commodities who process refined products and who hedge are able to reduce their cash expenditures substantially through hedging. Through the purchase of futures contracts they are able to assure themselves of a dependable supply at a stated price and quality before they will actually need to begin processing to meet a given forward sale. Their cost is a performance bond, the margin deposit. Grain and metal margins normally range from 5 to 15 percent of the actual market value of the commodity represented by the futures contract. Margins are subject to exchange-established minimum requirements and are kept consistent with the prevailing price risk.

Since the beginnings of futures markets, speculators have played an essential role in futures trading. The urge to study the supply and demand aspects of a particular commodity and put up venture capital in return for the chance to profit from price changes is an ancient impulse. Records of speculation by Roman citizens on the supply and price level of wheat during war predate the time of Julius Caesar. In an important case involving the Chicago Board of Trade before the U.S. Supreme Court in 1905, Chief Justice Oliver Wendell Holmes held that "people will endeavor to forecast the future and to make agreements according to their prophecy. Speculation of this kind by competent men is the self-adjustment of society to the probable. . . ."

Speculation has always been controversial, often because it is confused with gambling. However, gambling by definition involves the creation of risk solely for the purpose of making a wager. The risk of price changes in basic commodities is inherent and uncontrollable. In this sense, informed speculation in commodity futures contracts should not be considered gambling.

There is, further, a vital economic function provided by speculation in futures contracts. Professionals who seek to minimize risks through hedging in futures have a need to transfer that risk to others who are willing to and financially capable of bearing that risk. The latter are the speculators who possess venture capital— capital in excess of basic living requirements and prudent savings. Speculators hope to increase their capital through price forecasting and buying and selling futures contracts. If speculators were not willing to assume some of the risk inherent in the trading of basic commodities, futures markets would lack the liquidity—the ample presence of buyers and sellers—that makes them efficient hedging mechanisms. Lacking the ability to hedge, sellers of commodities would be forced to sell at higher prices in order to assure themselves a profit. Buyers of basic commodities would have to charge higher prices for the products they manufacture and sell in order to meet the higher costs of basic commodities and insure a profit. Without the presence of speculators and the liquidity they provide, international commerce in basic food, feedstuffs, and fiber could not be accomplished with the ease we enjoy today.

In recent years hedging opportunities have been created in areas well beyond the traditional agricultural markets. Among the newest futures markets are those in both long-term and short-term debt instruments. The development of these contracts and their applications will be outlined in the next chapter.

The evolution of interest rate futures

Recent fluctuations in interest rate levels have made the management of investment portfolios very difficult. It is no longer certain that a dollar invested today will be worth more tomorrow. Investments require diligent care by a sophisticated manager. Analysts must apply new strategies to improve their performance and simplify their jobs. Using interest rate futures to hedge a bond portfolio or transferring the risk of interest rate price movements has great appeal. Professional money managers are now investigating such possibilities from both an intellectual and a practical viewpoint in order to maximize their effectiveness.

Perhaps if we understand the reasons that made grain commodity contracts successful, we can better appreciate the potential value of an interest rate contract. For this purpose let us examine the evolution of the corn contract and then compare it to the beginning of the GNMA contract.

WHY THE CORN CONTRACT BECAME SUCCESSFUL

When the Illinois-Michigan Canal connecting the Great Lakes to the Mississippi River was completed in 1848, the corn belt came of age. No longer was the transportation of corn limited to expensive overland routes; corn could be transported inexpensively by ship to the populated areas of the East and Midwest. The only remaining problem was nature, which closed some inland waterways in early November. Often a late harvest could not be shipped to its destination until the following spring. This created a need for forward contracting. Simply stated, a *forward contract* is a promise to deliver a bushel of corn to a remote location at a future time. Initially, this time frame was four to six months. The terms and conditions of these contracts were not always standardized and they could be negotiated in many different ways. No one could be certain of obtaining the best price available at any given moment. The quality of products bought or sold was also problematic, since approximately 150 grades of corn were then in use.

As forward contracts, sometimes called time contracts, were used universally, brokers began to standardize the terms of delivery and grading. Thus, corn could be purchased throughout the year for May delivery in Chicago. This was good for the farmer, who was able to establish a price for something not yet owned; the farmer could determine future net profit. Payments were made more frequently than once a year, and harvest time became less important to a farmer's cash flow. Bills and accrued interest charges could be paid in a timely manner, thus increasing the farmer's lines of bank credit.

A further refinement of the forward contract was the development of a secondary market. The standardization of contract terms attracted speculators, who entered the corn market by buying and selling forward contracts among themselves. This provided additional liquidity to the market.

As mentioned earlier, when the Chicago Board of Trade (CBOT) was organized in 1848, it offered the advantage of centralized trading under controlled conditions. Trading by open outcry on the exchange floor made everyone aware of the value of a standard contract. Delivery instructions were uniformly precise, and misunderstanding was no longer a necessary evil associated with trading time contracts.

The establishment of a clearing corporation as part of a regulated exchange removed the danger of the soft contract. A clearing corporation is a nonprofit organization managed by its membership; its fiscal performance is guaranteed by the assets of its members. The corporation's responsibilities include establishing and monitoring both the trading regulations and the financial conditions of its membership, as well as daily margin calls. All positions of a clearing corporation member are marked to the market daily. A call for money is made if the member has a net negative balance. In addition, all trades conducted on the floor of the exchange are between a member and the clearing corporation. An individual no longer has to be concerned about who is on the other side of a transaction. Only the credit and reputation of the clearing corporation need be examined. Problems are no longer permitted to linger until the time a contract is due for settlement. Since daily maintenance margin calls are made, a failure due to the nonperformance of one party to a contract could cause a loss in proportion to only a one- or two-day price movement.

SIMILARITIES BETWEEN MORTGAGE ORIGINATION PRACTICES AND CORN PROCESSING

Money is often bought, sold, borrowed, and exchanged in ways analogous to agricultural products. Some transactions call for delayed deliveries or payment schedules that are exactly like forward contracts. By examining the characteristics of the mortgage industry, these similarities will become evident.

At the end of 1976, the amount of private mortgage debt exceeded the debt in all other private sectors, and it is still increasing at a rapid rate. Table 2-1 is a comparative listing, by sector, of outstanding debt in the United States at the end of 1977.

Residential mortgages are generally divided into single-family and commercial loan categories. Single-family loans can be subdivided into existing loans that result from refinancing transactions and loans for new construction. Refinancing transactions account for 60-75 percent of annual closings. Approximately 30 to 90 days elapse from the time an application for a mortgage is made until it is closed. New construction closings may take as long as one year. These transactions are analogous to forward contracts.

13

Table 2-1
Growth in selected types of credit
($ billions)

Type of credit	1950	1977*	Increase
Total credit outstanding	$427.0	$3,297.4	$2,870.4
Residential mortgage loans	54.5	760.6	706.1
Corporate and foreign bonds	39.2	387.1	347.9
State and local government obligations	24.4	265.1	240.7
Consumer credit	21.5	259.8	238.3
Mortgages on commercial properties	12.5	192.2	179.7
Federal debt	218.4	730.9	512.5

*Preliminary.
Sources: Federal Reserve Board; United States League of Savings Associations *Fact Book '78*, p. 26.

Since interest rates fluctuate, buyers generally try to obtain a reasonable mortgage commitment as a precondition for purchasing a new home. This is especially important when interest rates are rising and a buyer may have difficulty in qualifying for a satisfactory loan. The difference in the monthly payments of principal and interest for a 30-year, $60,000 mortgage closed at 9 percent versus one closed at 8 percent is $42.60.

Savings and loan associations must invest 82 percent of their assets in qualifying real estate-associated loans in order to be eligible for favorable tax treatment. Therefore, lenders who originate residential loans are also interested in obtaining future funding commitments. Often their cash flow, which is generated from regular monthly mortgage payments and payoffs, may be momentarily greater than the demand for new mortgage commitments in their operating area. Local interest rates also may be insufficient to generate desirable profit margins. These factors cause management to plan ahead 6 to 12 months in order to optimize their mortgage operation by issuing future commitments to purchase loans originated in other geographic areas.

In addition to thrift institutions, mortgage companies originate a large volume of single-family mortgages. Mortgage companies are generally highly leveraged intermediaries[1] that close loans in their

---

[1] See *Mortgage Banking*, 1976 Trend Report No. 20, issued by the Mortgage Bankers Association of America, p. 7.

names with the intent of making a profit by reselling them to permanent investors at a later date.[2] The longer they are exposed to interest rate fluctuations, the more difficult becomes their job. This is especially significant during periods of disintermediation, when the flow of savings into thrift institutions may level off or decrease, causing mortgage rates to rise.

The soft contract problem has also been a business hazard for a long time. When yield levels rise rapidly, lending institutions may have difficulty funding what they bought several months ago due to the effects of disintermediation. Likewise, mortgage originators may be exposed to large losses if they presell too many loans for forward delivery during times of high interest rates. If rates decrease before mortgage companies can originate these presold loans, they may have to pay more to buy the loans than their agreed upon selling price.

Grading residential real estate loans has always been a challenge. A mortgage application must be underwritten according to its location, property value, and the creditworthiness of the buyer. Perhaps the 150 varieties of corn are insignificant when compared with the infinite variables in real estate lending. The development of the Government National Mortgage Association (GNMA) mortgage backed security eliminated the necessity to grade this type of investment.

Their innovation paved the way for trading a mortgage interest rate futures contract on a regulated exchange. Its value can now be associated with the price of a GNMA security instead of an individual mortgage.

SIMILARITIES BETWEEN AGRICULTURAL COMMODITY CONTRACTS AND OTHER FINANCIAL INSTRUMENTS

Contracts that are not related to real estate, like U.S. government bonds, Treasury notes and bills, and commercial paper, are also

---

[2] These permanent investors include institutions that regularly invest assets in residential mortgages (i.e., savings and loan associations, mutual savings banks, life insurance companies).

traded on regulated commodity exchanges.[3] The economic values of these contracts are not associated with industry practices that require time contracts, but rather to securities that are exposed to tremendous price volatility. Weekly Treasury bill (T-bill) price changes in recent years approached $2,500 per $1 million, and are averaging $500. Table 2-2 displays these movements. These rapid gyrations make the ability to transfer price risks to a third party attractive to dealers, cash managers, investors, and speculators.

Table 2-2
Average weekly fluctuation in 13-week
Treasury bill auction rates

Year	Basis points	Year	Basis points
1965	3.3	1972	12.7
1966	7.3	1973	22.4
1967	11.4	1974	33.4
1968	10.4	1975	17.0
1969	11.1	1976	12.0
1970	17.2	1977	9.0
1971	15.8	1978	22.0

*Estimated.
Source: Chicago Mercantile Exchange, Treasury Bills Futures, p. 9.

Inventory hedging is definitely not the only justification for the existence of a futures contract. By illustration, the lumber industry has been using the commodity exchange for several years for transferring price risks to a third party. A price hedge executed by a plywood processor to establish a future cost has no impact on the inventory position.

Similarly, the sale of a T-bill contract on the futures market does little to protect the market value of an investment portfolio that does not include a T-bill. Such transactions merely establish price levels at which a trader feels confident that a profit can be generated from routine business transactions. Therefore, the hedge reflects a hedger's belief that current available futures prices are superior to those that can be expected for T-bill spot prices in the

---

[3] This is subject to the enforcement powers of the Commodity Futures Trading Commission.

future when they must be sold or bought in the cash market. One must remember that neither the purchase nor the sale of a financial instruments futures contract confers title or right to a security, mortgage, or note. Rather, it gives the owner of the contract the right to a profit or loss from a prospective price change. This is ideal for speculators and hedgers since bonds, notes, and money market instruments usually can be purchased more efficiently in the cash market at a later date. Additionally, the speculator often has no intention to make or take delivery of a security.

Rapid pricing changes have occurred in the past decade. From Figures 2-1, 2-2, and 2-3, it should be apparent that the new possibility of price hedging through transactions in interest rate futures contracts will provide welcome assistance to money managers in our inflationary climate.

Both the history of commodity trading and the current acceptance of interest rate futures contracts indicate that the concept of trading yields on a regulated exchange will be successful. Speculators like the idea because they are comfortable with the product. Hedgers use the contracts to simplify their task of managing large portfolios. Exchanges love interest rate contracts because they broaden their horizons into a world of new opportunities.

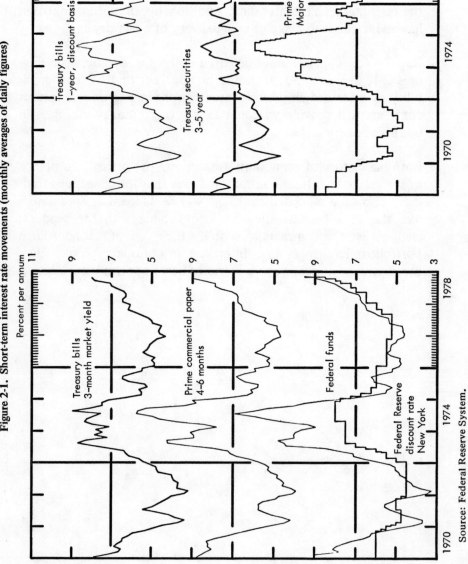

Figure 2-1. Short-term interest rate movements (monthly averages of daily figures)

Percent per annum

Treasury bills
1-year, discount basis

Treasury securities
3-5 year

Prime rate
Major banks

Percent per annum

Treasury bills
3-month market yield

Prime commercial paper
4-6 months

Federal funds

Federal Reserve
discount rate
New York

Source: Federal Reserve System.

Figure 2-2. Long-term interest rates (monthly averages)

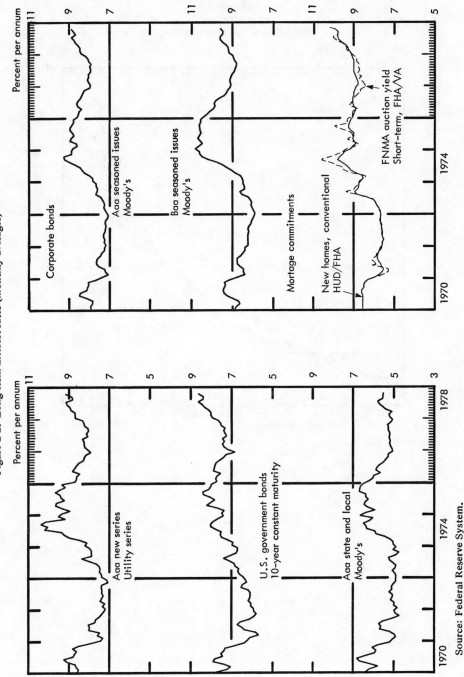

Source: Federal Reserve System.

Figure 2-3
Federal budget
(seasonally adjusted annual rates, quarterly

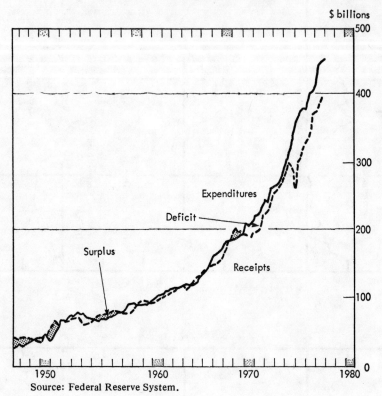

Source: Federal Reserve System.

What you need to know before trading on a commodity exchange

As of December 1978 there were seven interest rate futures contracts traded on regulated commodity exchanges in the United States. The Chicago Board of Trade (CBOT) trades the oldest GNMA mortgage interest rate contract, called a collateralized depository receipt (CDR). In addition it trades a revised GNMA contract that permits the direct delivery of a GNMA security, a U.S. Treasury bond, and a commercial paper contract. The Chicago Mercantile Exchange, hereafter referred to as the Merc, trades both a 90-day and a one-year Treasury bill contract. The American Commodity Exchange (ACE), established specifically to trade interest rate futures in 1978, began trading a direct-delivery GNMA contract on September 12, 1978.

Before entering any commodity trading arena, it is important to have a general knowledge of the regulations and terminology associated with each exchange and contract. In addition, one must understand the basic trading procedures and customs.

THE EXCHANGE

Commodity contracts can be traded only by members of a regulated exchange. This assures the investor of uniform trading rules,

21

contract terms, and fiscal responsibility. Commodity exchanges are nonprofit membership associations. Memberships can be held only by individuals, but corporate entities can be registered for specific privileges. The governing of an exchange is handled by a board of directors composed of exchange members and several outside directors. Its daily affairs are controlled by a professional staff, which takes care of the managerial and administrative needs. Currently the CBOT has more than 1,400 members and the Merc has approximately 500 full memberships. Both associations offer limited memberships to individuals who wish to restrict their trading activities to financial contracts.

In 1977 the CBOT sold 100 financial instrument memberships for $30,000 each. These memberships entitle the holders to the prorated privileges and responsibilities of a full membership but limit their activity to financial contracts traded in the South Room of the CBOT. The memberships are similar to International Monetary Market (IMM) memberships, which earlier became successful at the Merc.

The special memberships were designed to encourage dedicated investors to trade in the "money pits."[1] Without these individuals, an exchange would have to rely on its regular members to provide trading liquidity for interest rate contracts. This would be difficult, since floor brokers, speculators, and day traders usually specialize in only one commodity or a family of commodities. For example, if activity in the corn pit slows up at 11:00 A.M., it is not unusual to find corn traders active in the wheat pit. However, members are often reluctant to enter a foreign pit, such as a money pit, where they are relatively unfamiliar with the commodity being traded.

Special memberships have been overwhelmingly successful in achieving liquidity and increasing open positions. The latter is the criterion used to measure the success of a new contract. The daily trading volumes established by interest rate contracts have outper-

---

[1] A pit is a circular physical area where members gather who are interested in trading the same commodity.

formed those of most other commodities during similar periods of their life cycle.

Floor traders, brokers, scalpers

Members who trade on the floor of the exchange can be classified into three major categories. The first is the *floor broker*, who executes orders written by an account executive or a registered commodity representative. Floor brokers receive their instructions by telephone or teletype. Orders are then recorded and time stamped before they are executed. Floor brokers can be associated loosely with more than one member firm or can be an employee of a brokerage firm or commission merchant. Although the floor broker can talk directly to customers, the broker normally limits this activity to a few clients since it reduces executing efficiency for other customers. This type of broker seldom trades for a personal account. If the floor broker desires to take a position, he or she must excercise great care before filling a personal order at a specified price level.

The second type of broker is called a *speculator*. This person is critical in providing liquidity since speculators trade only for their personal accounts. Some observers have compared their function to that of a specialist on the floor of the New York Stock Exchange. The more speculators that function in a trading pit, the greater is the contract liquidity. Greater contract liquidity means that a larger order size can be executed without significantly affecting the execution price. Some speculators position only nearby contracts,[2] while others specialize in spreads.[3] The greater their capital, the greater is their contribution.

The third type of trader is a *day trader*. Day traders are sometimes referred to as "scalpers." The scalper usually will take a momentary position without regard to fundamentals or technical signals. Generally a day trader executes several dozen trades a day and has

---

[2] A nearby contract is the futures contract closest to expiration.

[3] See glossary in this chapter.

a flat position when trading stops. Although the scalper usually has a minimum of capital, he or she serves as a catalyst on the trading floor. All three categories of traders are equally important in maintaining contract liquidity and orderly price behavior.

Types of orders frequently processed

Market order. The most frequently used order is a market order. This instructs a floor broker to execute promptly an order at the most favorable price.

Limit order. A buy limit order prohibits the floor broker from paying more in the execution of a buy order than the limit set by the customer. If it is a sell limit order, the broker cannot sell for an amount less than that stipulated on the ticket. A limit order may be used to establish a new position or liquidate an old one. If the price is touched but the order cannot be executed, it does not become a market order. This can happen quite often in commodity trading because price moves are rapid and numerous floor brokers may have open orders to fill at an identical level. The limit order assures that a client will not pay more or sell for less than a specified amount.

If there is only one seller of ten contracts at a price of 97-00, and there are four buyers wishing to fill ten contracts at 97-00, only one order will be filled. If the following sale takes place at 97-01, the buy limit orders that were unfilled at 97-00 may never get filled. This is a significant difference from the stock market where all orders are channeled to one specialist and recorded in a time-received sequence that assures a buyer that the oldest buy order at a price of 97-00 is the first one filled. Under commodity trading rules, the investor cannot be assured that an order has been filled just because a price is displayed on a tape or on the inquiry station of a stock broker.

Stop orders. Stop orders are executed quite differently than limit orders. A buy stop order is usually placed above the current market price and will become a market order if the price is touched.

Its use is illustrated by a client who determines that a technical buy signal exists for the September 1978 long-term government contract at 95-18, although it is currently trading at 95-01. The customer instructs the broker to enter a buy stop order at 95-18 for one contract and mark it good until canceled. The broker now is directed to buy one September 1978 long-term government contract after the price of 95-18 has been touched. The order can be executed at, above, or below 95-18 until it is specifically canceled. If the ticket is marked as a day order, it can be executed only if 95-18 is touched during that session. A sell stop order is placed below the current price level and also converts to a market order when the order price is touched.

Miscellaneous techniques. A stop limit order is a more sophisticated limit order. It instructs the floor broker to execute an order if the price is touched but restricts execution to a price within the broker's stop instructions. Perhaps a client wants the advantages of a limit buy order but does not wish to be deprived of an execution by a small price variation. The broker could use a buy stop limit order to specify a price range within which it is acceptable to execute the order. This is a restricted version of a buy stop order.

Orders can also be placed with instruction to be executed at the opening or closing of a trading session without regard to the price.

There are other exotic ways of entering orders into the system, but those reviewed should satisfy the needs of most hedgers and speculators. Most speculators will find choosing a trend sufficiently challenging without compounding the chore by selecting specific execution prices. Market, limit, and stop orders make up the largest percentage of transactions.

The order-processing cycle

Once a commodity futures order is entered by a customer, the broker must get the instruction to the trading floor of the appropriate exchange. Transmitting through either automated equipment or clerks in back offices, the broker sends commodity orders to the appropriate order desk. In some cases, customers may be allowed to call directly to an exchange and place their orders with the trading floor personnel.

After the order is received on the floor of the exchange, it is printed on a standard format and time stamped. The stamp indicates when the order was received on the trading floor. The "hard copy" is sent by runner to the designated trading area, or pit, for that commodity. It is given to the floor broker who is selected by the firm to execute its orders in that pit.

If the order is "at the market," it is executed immediately, assuming the market is not "limit bid" for buy orders or "limit sellers" for sell orders.[4] Usually, the runner who takes the order to the pit waits while a market order is being filled and then returns it to his or her firm for a confirmation transmittal to the appropriate branch office or customer.

When the order has a "price limit," the floor broker files it in his or her order deck. Limit orders are filed by price, with the transaction being completed as the market moves within the parameters designated by the customer. If a broker holds more than one order at the same price, the orders must be executed in the order in which they were received. Because of varying degrees of efficiency on the part of brokerage firms, orders are not necessarily received by floor brokers in the same time sequence that they are placed by different customers. Thus the sequence in which orders are filled on the floor does not necessarily reflect the time sequence in which they were received from customers.

GLOSSARY FOR INTEREST RATE FUTURES

Every profession or trade has its own jargon, and commodity trading is no exception. Its language is not difficult to understand, but it is confusing when one interprets the terms as they are used on a stock exchange. Several words that are used in both an equity and a commodity transaction have totally different meanings in the two contexts.

---

[4] See the glossary below.

The following terms are frequently used in connection with commodity trading and require your review.

Arbitrage. Usually associated with a transaction in the bond market in which two different bonds are positioned simultaneously. One security is purchased and the other is sold. These positions are reversed simultaneously. The objective of the transaction is to profit from a temporary price discrepancy between the two debt instruments when they return to a normal price relationship.

Basis. The difference between the immediate cash price of a security and the price of the nearby interest rate futures contract.

Basis point (BP). A measurement of the change in yield levels for fixed income securities. One basis point equals 1/100 of 1 percent.

Broad tape. News wires that carry exchange prices and trading information to the outside world.

Broker. A person paid a fee or commission for acting as an agent in making contracts or sales. Also a floor broker in commodities futures trading who executes orders on the trading floor of an exchange.

Brokerage fee. The same as a commission in the stock market; however, the fee charged per contract is paid only once when the contract is closed out by an offsetting transaction or delivery.

Buy-in (offset). An equal and opposite transaction to an earlier position, which eliminates the customer's position. When this transaction has been concluded, a net profit or loss can be computed.

Cash commodity. The actual security, bill, or note that would be eligible for delivery if one wished to satisfy an open obligation without offsetting the position. Only a small percentage of contracts are ever satisfied by delivery.

Cash forward market. A market made by GNMA dealers who trade in GNMA mortgage-backed securities from 30 to 180 days in the future.

CFTC. Commodity Futures Trading Commission, an agency controlled by the Secretary of Agriculture and with responsibility for monitoring all commodity exchanges.

Cheap. Bond traders' vernacular describing a fixed income security that is underpriced in relation to other bonds with similar characteristics. An overpriced bond is called "rich."

Clearinghouse. A corporation closely associated with a commodity exchange through which all futures contracts are made and offset or completed through actual delivery. All financial obligations related to the margins associated with a trade are monitored by this organization. A clearinghouse is owned by its membership.

Collateralized depository receipts (CDRs). The CDR GNMA mortgage interest rate futures contract traded on the CBOT does not allow for direct delivery of GNMA certificates in the settlement of a futures position. Instead, the contract calls for the delivery of a negotiable instrument called a collateralized depository receipt. A CDR is a document prepared, signed, and dated by a depository bank to reflect the fact that a seller has placed a $100,000 minimum principal balance for GNMAs with an 8% coupon or equivalent, for safekeeping on the date so indicated. This is similar to a warehouse receipt.

Contract regulations. Knowledge of contract regulations is imperative for a hedger and important to a speculator. These regulations define which securities can be delivered to satisfy a position, when delivery can be made, and who can do it. This is expecially important to GNMA traders since some contracts permit premium bonds to be delivered without par stops. When a person with a long position stands for delivery, he or she should expect to receive the cheapest commodity that can be purchased to satisfy an obligation.

Correlation coefficient. Correlation is the degree to which yield and price fluctuations of one security or money market instrument are reflected by another such security or money market instrument. The more accurate the correlation, the larger is the correlation coefficient. A correlation coefficient of 100 denotes a perfect relationship.

Cross hedge. The buying or selling of an interest rate futures contract to protect the value of a cash position of a similar, but not identical, instrument. This type of hedging is a measured risk since the outcome of such a transaction is a function of the price correlation of the securities being hedged. At any given moment it is conceivable that a negative correlation could exist between two unlike instruments despite the presence of a strong positive correlation over an extended period of time.

Current delivery (month). The futures contract that is closest to expiration. This contract is sometimes referred to as the *nearby month.*

Day trades. Trades that are established and offset on the same day. These are usually conducted by scalpers or customers who are active speculators. Day trades incur a significantly lower brokerage fee than regular trades.

Delivery month. T-bills, GNMAs, long-term government securities, and commercial paper contracts are posted every quarter for periods longer than two years. The delivery month is the calendar month during which these contracts mature and "go off the board."

Delivery notice. A formal procedure that must be followed if a position open in the delivery month is to be satisfied by the delivery of a permissible security as defined in the contract.

Discount price. The price of a bond trading at less than par. (Par is 100 cents on a dollar of its face value.)

First day of notice. The first day on which a seller can notify a buyer that he or she wishes to deliver a cash commodity against an open futures position. This procedure is regulated by the clearing corporation.

GNMA. Government National Mortgage Association, an agency under the Department of Housing and Urban Development that has the jurisdiction to approve the issue of mortgage-backed securities that are fully guaranteed for repayment of principal and interest by the U.S. Treasury, as described in the standard prospectus for HUD 1717, 3/73. As of December 1978, more than $65 billion GNMAs have been issued, carrying various coupon rates from 6.5 to 9 percent.

Hedging. A technique used by institutions that substitute the sale of an interest rate futures contract for the sale of the actual cash security. Success is related to the price correlation of the futures contract with that of the security being hedged. Hedging can also refer to a buying transaction in which the actual purchase of a security in the cash market is deferred by purchasing an interest rate futures contract. (Also see *Cross hedge.*)

Last trading day. Day on which trading ceases for an expiring contract, sometimes called a *nearby contract.*

Limit bid or limit sell moves (daily trading limits). Refers to the maximum price move a contract can experience during one trading session before it is stopped from trading, as explicitly defined in the contract. After a contract stops trading, it can be reopened if someone is willing to trade above or below the daily price limit at a later time during the trading session.

Limit order. An order in which the customer designates either a price limit or a time limit before execution is possible.

Liquidity. A term used to describe the price sensitivity of a contract. Liquidity also can be measured by the size of an order that can be executed without significantly affecting the execution price.

Long. A buyer of a contract. If not offset, the long position will take delivery of a contract on its expiration date.

Margins. Several types of margins are used in trading commodities. A security deposit guaranteeing performance is called the *initial margin.* It is required to open an account traded on a regulated exchange. All member firms must conform with this regulation before an account can begin trading. An initial margin can be deposited in T-bills.

The *maintenance margin* is a level below which the initial margin is not permitted to float. A maintenance margin balance is computed by debiting or crediting the daily price movements of a contract to the intial margin balance. If the price behaves favorably for the contract holder, he or she builds a surplus that can be withdrawn. If the price movement goes against the contract holder, the initial margin is reduced by the appropriate amount based on a daily mark to market.

Mark to market. An arithmetic procedure conducted daily by a brokerage house for each open account; the procedure debits or credits the available balance of the account by the sum of the dollar change in value of open contracts resulting from price movements occurring during the last trading session.

Market order. An order to buy or sell a contract immediately at the best price.

Nearbys. The nearest actively traded month in a selected commodity contract.

Offset. See *Buy-in.*

Open interest. A figure that refers to the total number of contracts not offset or satisfied by a delivery for a given contract. The larger the number, the more liquid is the contract. Thus, it would be prohibitive to buy or sell 100 contracts of a specific month if there was an open interest of only 124.

Open outcry. A technique of public auction used to make bids or offers in a pit. Brokers cannot buy and sell positions they own without availing themselves of this procedure.

Pit. A trading area on the floor of a commodity exchange where all trades associated with a specific contract are made.

Point. An amount equal to 1 percent of the principal amount of a fixed income security or mortgage. Points are computed when a bond or mortgage is bought or sold. They are used to alter the yields of bonds or mortgages to current market rates.

Position. An open market commitment.

Pricing. GNMAs and government securities prices are expressed in points and 32ds, as in 97-01, with digits to right of the dash being 32ds. The points reflect a percentage of par, thus 100-00 is 100 percent of par. A price of 94-08 would indicate a price of $94\frac{8}{32}$ percent of par. Price changes do not occur with the same magnitude as yield changes; there is no straight-line relationship. The remaining maturity of a bond has a major effect on the relative changes of prices and yields.

Reporting limit. Sizes of positions set by an exchange or the CFTC above which brokerage firms must report all open customer positions to the designated authority. These limits are more stringent for speculative positions than for hedge transactions.

Repurchase agreement (repo). The selling of a security by a dealer to another party at the same time that the other party enters into an agreement to resell the securities to the dealer at a predetermined price and date.

Reverse repurchase agreement (reverse repo). The sale of a security by an investor or mortgage banker to a dealer while the investor simultaneously agrees to repurchase the security at a specific price and date. It is used to temporarily borrow against collateral.

Rich. See *Cheap.*

Short. A sale. It is also associated with an open interest rate contract that permits the contract holder to satisfy a position by delivering an appropriate security or collateralized depository receipt. It can be offset through an equal and opposite trade.

Speculator. A trader in futures contracts who attempts to profit from anticipated price changes.

Spread (straddle). The simultaneous purchase and sale of different contract months of the same commodity contract. This usually is executed when the price relationship between contract months is deemed to be abnormal. The positions are simultaneously offset when the price relationships return to a normal basis. This trading technique is similar to an arbitrage.

Spot price. The current cash market price of a security in the immediate market.

SUMMARY OF INTEREST RATE CONTRACTS[5]

GNMA collateralized depository receipt (CBOT)

Deliverable commodity

Any GNMA security can be delivered by a regular originator to an approved depository bank. The securities may be of different pools and coupon rates. The depository bank issues a collateralized depository receipt (CDR) to the investor with the long

---

[5] Summaries of exchange regulations prepared by Dean Witter Reynolds, Inc., in existence on December 1978. They are subject to change.

position. These CDRs may be surrendered for GNMA securities. This cycle requires 15 business days.

Exchange-designated coupon rates	Nominal 8 percent coupon with yield maintenance provisions subject to deliverable commodity rule.
Delivery	
Notice dates	CDR deliverable through last day of month.
Pools	Any number of pools per contract may be delivered.
Months	March, June, September, and December.
Matching shorts with longs	The clearing corporation matches CDRs after the investor with the short position gives delivery notice.
Trading hours	8:30-2:45 CST.
Price quotations	On a percentage of par, with minimum price fluctuations 1/32 of a point ($31.25 per contract).
Daily price limits	Normally 24/32 above and below the previous day's settlement price; increased to 36/32 when variable price limits are in effect. Price limits do not apply to trading in contracts for delivery during a specific month on or after the first notice day for deliveries during that month.

GNMA certificate delivery (CBOT)

Deliverable commodity	Coupons that may be delivered against a futures contract in a given delivery month are designated as follows:

1. Any coupon at or below the current production rate is deliverable. If the current production rate is lower than the previous production rate, then the previous production rate is also deliverable in the next three months following the month in which the production rate was lowered.
2. The above is subject to the provision that no substitution of coupon is made for any delivery date until 45 days after the effective date of the rate change. That is, if the current production rate is changed, certificates bearing the new coupon rate are not deliverable on the Board of Trade futures contract until 45 days after the new coupon rate is in effect. The one exception to this rule is the delivery of a

	new issue dated and issued after the date of record of the rate change and bearing the new rate.
Exchange-designated coupon rates	Nominal 8 percent coupon with yield maintenance provision subject to deliverable commodity rule. The designated coupon rate can be changed to another rate by the exchange before a new contract is posted.
Delivery	
Notice dates	The position day (day notice is given) is three business days prior to the delivery day. Delivery day is the 16th day of the delivery month.
Pools	No more than one pool may be delivered per contract.
Months	March, June, September, and December.
Matching shorts with longs	A designated bank agent matches long and short positions and splits certificates when necessary.
Trading hours	8:30-2:45 CST.
Price quotations	On a percentage of par, with minimum price fluctuations 1/32 of a point ($31.25 per contract).
Daily price limits	Normally 24/32 above and below the previous day's settlement price; increased to 36/32 when variable price limits are in effect. Price limits do not apply to trading in contracts for delivery during a specific month on or after the first notice day for deliveries during that month.

GNMA certificate delivery (ACE)

Deliverable commodity	GNMA certificates bearing either the exchange-designated coupon rate or any lower or higher coupon rate. A GNMA coupon rate that is higher than the exchange-designated coupon interest rate is not deliverable if the adjusted firm yield maintenance price is more than 100 percent of par, except when such coupon rate represents the current production. In the event of a change in the FHA/VA mortgage ceiling rate, previous production rate coupons are deliverable for up to 45 days following the next delivery date.

Exchange-designated coupon rates	The designated contract coupon rate for each month is 8 percent. The designated rate can be changed to another rate by the exchange before a new contract rate is posted.
Delivery Notice dates	Any open contracts must be settled on the fifth business day following the last day of trading. The last day of trading is the third Tuesday of the month.
Pools	No more than two pools can be delivered with each multiple of ten contracts. Fewer than ten contract deliveries must be from the same pool.
Months	February, May, August, and November plus every current month.
Matching shorts with longs	Clearing corporation matches positions and orders members to split certificates when necessary.
Trading hours	9:30-3:45 EDT.
Price quotations	On a percentage of par, with minimum price fluctuations 1/32 of a point ($31.25 per contract).
Daily price limits	Normally, 24/32 above and below the previous day's settlement price; increased to 36/32 when variable price limits are in effect. Price limits do not apply to trading in contracts for delivery during a specific month on or after the first notice day for deliveries during that month.

Long-term U.S. Treasury bond futures

Deliverable grade	U.S. Treasury bonds that if callable, are not callable for at least 15 years from date of delivery, or if not callable, do not mature for at least 15 years from date of delivery. All bonds delivered on a contract must be of the same issue.
Basic contract trading unit	Bonds with a face value at maturity of $100,000 and a coupon rate of 8 percent. Bonds with coupon rates other than 8 percent are deliverable at discounts for bonds with coupons less than 8 percent and at premiums for bonds with coupons more than 8 percent.

Delivery method	By book-entry system in accordance with Department of Treasury Circular 300, available from any Federal Reserve Bank. Accrued interest is prorated in accordance with Department of Treasury Circular 300.
Price quotations	On percentage of par, with minimum price fluctuations 1/32 of a point ($31.25 per contract).
Daily price limits	Normally 32/32 above and below the previous day's settlement price; increased to 48/32 when variable price limits are in effect. Price limits do not apply to trading in contracts for delivery during a specific month on or after the first notice day for deliveries during that month.

90-day Treasury bill futures contract

Deliverable grade	A U.S. Treasury bill having a face value of $1 million and a maturity of 90 or 91 days.
Basic contract trading unit	All bills should be maturing in 90 days. At a seller's option a delivery unit may be composed of U.S. Treasury bills bearing maturities of 91 or 92 days. All bills in a delivery unit must bear uniform maturity dates. Payments are made in accordance with the provisions of Rule 1503 F, reflecting the maturity date of the U.S. Treasury bills actually delivered.
Delivery method Seller's duties	The clearing member representing the seller delivers to the IMM Clearinghouse by 12:00 noon (Chicago time) on the last day of trading a seller's delivery commitment indicating a Chicago bank, registered with the IMM and a member of the Federal Reserve System, and the name of the account from which the delivery unit will be transferred. By 11:00 A.M. (Chicago time) on the day of delivery, the seller delivers to a Chicago bank, registered with the IMM and a member of the Federal Reserve System, selected by the buyer, a U.S. Treasury bill(s) maturing in 90 days, with a face value at maturity of $1 million.
Buyer's duties	The clearing member representing the buyer delivers to the clearinghouse by 12:00 noon (Chicago time) on the last day of trading a

buyer's delivery commitment including the buyer's name and account number and the name of a Chicago bank, registered with the IMM and a member of the Federal Reserve System, to which the delivery unit should be transferred, and by 11:00 A.M. (Chicago time) on the day of delivery presents to the selling clearing member's bank or its designated agent a wire transfer of federal funds for the net invoicing price.

Price quotations	Price quoted in terms of the IMM index. (Example: A T-bill yield of 5.20 is quoted as 94.80.) Minimum price fluctuations of the IMM index are in multiples of 0.01 ($25.00). The minimum fluctuation is equal to one basis point.
Daily price limits	There is no trading at a price more than 0.50 (50 basis points) above or below the preceding day's settlement price except as provided by Rule 1508 (expanded daily price limits), and on the last day of trading when there is no limit.

One-year U.S. Treasury bills

Deliverable contract	Each futures contract is for U.S. Treasury bills of one-year maturity with a face value of $250,000 at maturity.
Delivery Notice day	Futures trading terminates on the Monday following the first one-year T-bill auction held in a contract month, unless that day is an IMM or Illinois bank holiday. In that case trading terminates on the previous Friday.
Delivery days	Par deliveries are made on the Tuesday following the termination of trading. If that day is an IMM or Illinois bank holiday, deliveries are on the next business day common to the IMM and Illinois banks.
Pricing	Prices are quoted in terms of the IMM index. This represents the difference between the actual T-bill yield and 100.00.
Daily price range	Trading is limited to 50 basis points (0.50) above or below the preceding day's settlement price except as provided by Rule 3208 (expanded daily price limits) and on the last day of trading when there is no limit.

Minimum price fluctuations	Price fluctuations are in multiples of 0.01. This minimum price move has a value of $25 per contract.

Commercial paper contract[6]

Deliverable grade of paper	Commercial paper that matures on a business day not more than 90 days from the date of delivery of the financial receipt in the futures market, and that (1) is rated A-1 by Standard & Poor's Corporation, (2) is rated P-1 by Moody's Investors Service, Inc., and (3) is approved as deliverable by the CBOT.
Basic contract trading unit	Commercial paper with a face value at maturity of $1 million.
Delivery method	By financial receipt. This is a document signed by an approved vault to warrant that $1 million face value of contract-grade commercial paper has been deposited with it in safekeeping. Financial receipts may be surrendered for commercial paper. Under the contract, there is no adjustment for delivery of commercial paper with less than 90 days outstanding.
Price quotations	On an annualized discount basis, with minimum price fluctuations of one basis point (1/100 of 1 percent of $1 million, or $25 per contract).
Daily price limits	Normally 25 basis points above and below the previous day's settlement price; increased to 38 basis points when variable price limits are in effect. Price limits do not apply to trading in contracts for delivery during a specific month on or after the first notice day for deliveries during that month.
Unique feature	The sale of a futures contract (going short) is defined as the commitment to deliver a cash loan. The purchase of a futures contract (going long) is defined as the commitment to pay in commercial paper. This is the inverse from other interest rate contracts.

---

[6] As of December 1978 this contract is being significantly redesigned. A 30-day commercial paper contract is soon to be posted.

Pricing fundamentals for fixed income securities and interest rate futures

The purpose of this chapter is to describe and review some basic techniques of pricing debt instruments and interest rate futures contracts. These concepts become the foundation for understanding the importance of their price correlations.

THE SIGNIFICANCE OF CORRELATIONS

Before pursuing the study of interest rate futures contracts, we must assume that interest rate futures contracts maintain a satisfactory price correlation with like securities traded in the cash market. For example, the price movement of the 90-day T-bill futures contract must be in the same direction and have the same approximate magnitude as the price of a 90-day Treasury bill.

A review of the historical price movements of GNMAs, U.S. government bonds, T-bills, and commercial paper is, therefore, desirable since the usefulness of an interest rate futures contract becomes questionable if its correlations to cash prices disappear for extended periods.

TRADING FIXED INCOME SECURITIES

Bonds are referred to as "fixed income securities" by money managers and bond dealers because the term defines a fixed annual income stream. If a bond is issued with a 6 percent coupon, it pays 6 percent interest to maturity. If a bond is issued in denominations of $1,000, a par buyer pays $1,000. When the price of the bond is less than $1,000, the bond is referred to as a *discount* bond. If the purchase price is more than $1,000, the bond is called a *premium* bond. Whether a bond is resold at more or less than its initial face value is a function of the interest rate level that exists when the sale takes place.

The remaining life of a bond is called its *maturity* and is quoted in years. The maturity date indicates to the holder of a bond when the principal will be fully repaid. Most bonds issued today carry initial maturities of 10 to 30 years and pay interest semiannually.

Bond buyers share the same objectives as investors who trade stocks. They hope to buy low and sell high! In the stock market, this can be accomplished by buying an IBM share at 240 and selling it at 285. When trading bonds, this relationship is similar. Bonds should be purchased when yields are high and prices low, and sold when yields are low and prices high. This is depicted in Figure 4-1.

Investors who buy a fixed income stream must use pricing to equalize bond yields. This strategy permits a bond trader to adjust the yield of any fixed income security to a current yield level. For example, assume that a AAA utility issues a $1,000 noncallable bond with a maturity of 25 years carrying a coupon of 8 percent. If interest rate levels for this type of bond are at 8 percent on the day of issue, the bond will be sold at par, or a price equal to 100 percent of its face value. If the buyer wishes to resell this security at a later date when interest rate levels have increased to 8.5 percent, he or she will receive a discounted price of less than 100 percent. The actual price (percent of par) can be manually computed only for a perpetual bond by dividing the coupon of the bond by the current yield level. In dealing with other than perpet-

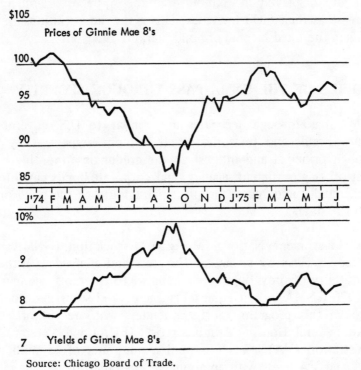

Figure 4-1
Price and yield chart for a typical fixed income security

Source: Chicago Board of Trade.

ual bonds, the investor must refer to an appropriate yield book for establishing precise pricing. A detailed discussion of how to use a yield book is found in Chapter 5.

TRADING TREASURY BILLS

Treasury bills (T-bills) are normally bought and sold by money market dealers and commercial banks. Their rates are quoted on the basis of a bank discount rate, which is also the T-bill yield. Both terms are used interchangeably. Essentially, the bank discount rate is the difference between the face value of a bill and its market value on an annualized basis. Therefore, the T-bill yield must be converted to a bond yield in order to make comparisons.

The formulas for calculating discount yield and equivalent bond yield are displayed in Exhibit A in the Appendix. T-bill prices decrease as their yield increases. This is the same relationship that exists in the fixed income or bond market.

PROFILE OF THE GNMA PASS-THROUGH SECURITY

GNMA pass-through securities are similar to U.S. government agency bonds and treasuries in all but one respect. They pass through principal and interest to the holder on a monthly basis. Most other government, agency, and corporate bonds pay interest semiannually and repay the principal amount of the bond on its maturity date.

The Government National Mortgage Association (GNMA) was created in 1968 by an act of Congress and charged with the responsibility of providing federal support to the mortgage market. In 1970 GNMA initiated the mortgage-backed securities program. Through this program, mortgage lenders who are authorized to make Federal Housing Administration (FHA) and Veterans Administration (VA) loans can pool a minimum of $1 million of FHA and VA loans with an approved custodian bank. The custodian bank certifies to GNMA that all mortgages in the pool are properly executed and calculates the face amount of their combined mortgage balances. Upon receipt of this certification, GNMA gives its approval for the mortgage lender to issue a GNMA pass-through security for a value equal to the mortgage balance of the collateralized loans.

The term *pass through*, which is associated with a GNMA, refers to the technique of passing through the principal and interest collected on the underlying mortgages on a monthly basis. This amount can come from regular mortgage payments, accelerated payoffs, or foreclosure transactions. The issuer must pass through to the security holder monthly, whether collected or not, an amount equal to the 30-year amortization schedule of the FHA/VA mortgages used to collateralize the GNMA security. (See Exhibit B.) This performance is guaranteed by GNMA.

As of December 1978, approximately $65 billion of GNMA pass-

42

throughs have been issued since the program began in 1970.[1] Currently, their ownership is distributed in the following manner.

	Percentage of outstanding ownerships
Mortgage bankers	18
Savings and loan associations	15
Mutual savings banks	12
Pension funds	11
Commercial banks	6
Credit unions	3
Individuals	1
Others	34

Mortgage banking organizations are the largest group of GNMA issuers. Similarly, thrift institutions are the major investors in GNMAs, owning nearly 30 percent of the total outstanding pass-throughs. Two reasons for their active participation are:

1. GNMAs are qualifying investments for tax purposes.
2. An active secondary cash market is available and permits thrifts to buy and sell GNMAs according to their current liquidity requirements.

These needs cannot be met as easily with insured or conventional whole loan purchases.[2]

A substantial over-the-counter market has developed in GNMA securities since the pass-through program was initiated. In the secondary market, GNMA pass-throughs are traded with bid-ask (buy-sell) spreads of 2/32 to 4/32.[3] The daily volume of trading often exceeds $1 billion.

PRICING GNMA PASS-THROUGH SECURITIES

The GNMA mortgage backed security is the only government-guaranteed bond that is traded in an active cash forward market for 180 days. Securities can be purchased or sold for future deliv-

---

[1] See GNMA Monthly Activity Report, December 30, 1978.

[2] Prior to 1974 most mortgages were sold individually as whole loans to permanent investors.

[3] The price difference between the purchase and sale price at any given moment.

ery dates without the customary margin requirements. This practice is under continuous review by numerous regulatory agencies since both customers and dealers are exposed to soft contracts—called fails. Transactions are processed on the trade date but are not paid for until the settlement day.

The price level of GNMAs available for immediate delivery, sometimes called *nearby*, can be validated by two distinct criteria. The oldest technique is to compare the GNMA price with the Federal National Mortgage Association (FNMA) price obtainable in the regular biweekly FNMA auction.[4] Another technique is to compare GNMA prices with the prices of other government securities having similar maturities.

The FNMA auction is conducted by FNMA for its authorized servicers. It is a private corporation, chartered by Congress, and is wholly owned by stockholders whose purpose is to provide a national secondary market for government-backed and conventional mortgages. Through its secondary market operations, FNMA provides a source of liquidity for mortgage lenders throughout the country. By issuing forward purchase commitments, FNMA assures approved FHA/VA lenders that a permanent investor is always available at some price for mortgages originated, regardless of the prevailing money and housing market conditions.

An approved mortgage originator who participates in these auctions may bid either competitively for a maximum of $3 million per bid or noncompetitively for $250,000. Since delivery is not mandatory, the seller always retains the option of selling his or her production (sometimes referred to as *origination*) as a GNMA modified pass-through security. The comparison at the top of page 45 outlines the primary features of both programs.

Most mortgage originators sell their production in the most favorable available outlet based on price. At various times during the past years, the FNMA auction yields less the GNMA securities yields (based on the immediate bid price) have fluctuated between 40 and 100 basis points. Figure 4-2 illustrates these spreads.

---

[4] FNMA auction results are publicly released every other Tuesday.

	GNMA security	FNMA auction
Price	Determined by individual GNMA dealers	Established by auction results
Delivery time	Dealer's discretion	120 days
Annual servicing income . .	0.44% of mortgage balance	0.375% of mortgage balance
Underwriting	Basic FHA/VA regulations	Basic FHA/VA regulations
Investor relationships. . . .	No exposure to servicing cancellations or fee renegotiations unless specific cause can be shown	Formal, open to renegotiation of servicing agreements and cancellation of contracts
Cash flow	May require additional funds if delinquencies become significant	Passes through only what has been collected
Commitment fees.	None, but being reviewed	0.5 point, nonrefundable, if successful bidder
Mandatory delivery.	Yes	No

The lower the GNMA yield, the higher is the GNMA price. Since the originator must sell loans at a maximum price, the greater the yield spread between the GNMA security and the FNMA alternative, the more favorable is the GNMA market.

A second method for establishing an appropriate GNMA price is the historical spread relationship between GNMAs and other gov-

Figure 4-2
Spread: FNMA FHA/VA yields less GNMA securities yields*

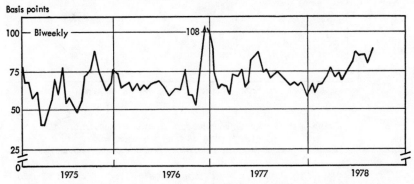

*FNMA FHA/VA yields are averages for the four-month commitments issued in the biweekly Free Market System auction. GNMA yields are based on bid prices (immediate delivery) obtained from three New York dealers as of close of business on the Friday preceding the FNMA auction.
Source: MBA Economics Department, Federal National Mortgage Association.

ernment or agency bonds. Price and yield spread analyses are readily available. Thus a GNMA 8.00 percent current price can be compared with the price of an 8.00 percent Treasury bond with a maturity of August 1986, or the price of a 7.875 percent Treasury bond with a maturity of 2005. Figure 4-3 portrays an arbitrage trading opportunity between GNMA 8's and Treasury 8's of 1986.

This type of sector analysis has liberated the GNMA security from prices that are determined solely by a FNMA auction. GNMA prices can now deviate from FNMA auction results when arbitrage

Figure 4-3
Price spread relationship between GNMA 8's and Treasury 8's of 1986

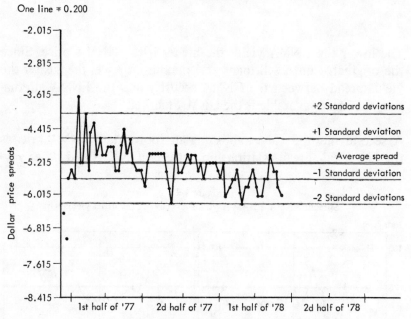

Graph of the weekly dollar price spreads of two issues from
December 3, 1976, to June 2, 1978

	CUSIP number	Quality	Description or name of issuer	Cou-pon	Maturity date	Price as of 6/02/78
First issue	382997AP	NR-NR	GNMA	8.000	12/15/09	91.994
Second issue. . . .	912827FW		U.S. Treasury	8.000	8/15/86	97.937
The spread between the prices is						−5.943

Source: Docuswap, A Service of Cunningham & Company, Detroit, Michigan.

opportunities between GNMAs and other sectors of the government bond market are available.

The 12-year average life

Whether the FNMA auction is used to determine a fair price for a GNMA security or whether a sector analysis is made between a GNMA security and another government bond, it is imperative to understand the 12-year life associated with a GNMA security.

The 12-year average life was selected from the data base of FHA single-family mortgages. The 30-year FHA historical data base combines mortgages with various terms and coupon rates. The data base indicates a half-life for FHA loans of 11.1 years and a principal weighted life of 12.5 years.[5] For this purpose of measurement, a half-life refers to the dollar half-life. Another way of expressing this is to state that at half-life, 50 percent of the mortgage balance has been repaid. The remaining balance is assumed to be paid in one lump sum on a date called the principal weighted life. In reality it is possible to have one loan in a pool pay off one month after the security is issued and another loan remain active for the full term of the mortgage. Tables 4-1 and 4-2 illustrate average mortality rates of FHA mortgages.

The half-life and principal weighted life are less than the maturity of the underlying mortgages for the following reasons:

1. Payoffs due to relocation and upgrading of housing.
2. Payoffs due to change in lifestyle as a result of death or divorce.
3. Payoffs due to burn mortgage syndrome.
4. Foreclosures.

Table 4-3 depicts the principal cash flow that can be expected from a GNMA if it continues to prepay at the rate computed during its first four years of life.

Practical experience has shown that GNMA securities with high coupons and with underlying mortgages located in transient com-

---

[5] See Michael Waldman, *Average Life of Mortgage Related Instruments* (New York: Salomon Brothers, December 8, 1977).

Table 4-1
FHA mortgage mortality table*
(original term 26-30 years)

This FHA-prepared mortality table includes all insured mortgages with original terms of 26 to 30 years. The vast majority are 30-year mortgages. Shown below is the table computed in 1977 based on all mortgages insured from 1957 through 1975.

The left-hand column shows the number of mortgages living at the beginning of each year, starting with the radix of 100,000 mortgages. The right-hand column shows the number of mortgages dying each year by prepayment.

The figures through 19 years are based on actual experience; the remaining figures are estimates.

Years	Living at first of year	Prepaid during year	Years	Living at first of year	Prepaid during year
1	1.00000	0.00813	17	0.44448	0.01966
2	0.99187	0.02941	18	0.42482	0.01728
3	0.96246	0.04039	19	0.40754	0.02478
4	0.92207	0.04541	20	0.38276	0.02395
5	0.87666	0.04694	21	0.35881	0.02307
6	0.82972	0.04720	22	0.33574	0.02217
7	0.78252	0.04488	23	0.31357	0.02127
8	0.73764	0.04194	24	0.29230	0.02033
9	0.69570	0.03860	25	0.27197	0.01941
10	0.65710	0.03626	26	0.25256	0.01846
11	0.62084	0.03446	27	0.23410	0.01753
12	0.58638	0.03189	28	0.21657	0.01660
13	0.55449	0.03124	29	0.19997	0.01568
14	0.52325	0.02909	30	0.18429	0.01429
15	0.49416	0.02650	31	0.17000	0.00000
16	0.46766	0.02318			

*This table is composed of predominately low-rate mortgages, which show slower amortization rates than current mortgages.
Source: FHA, Boston: Financial Publishing Company, Publication 715.

munities, such as California, pay off most rapidly. If a bond is purchased at a discount, the investor benefits from an accelerated payoff rate.[6] Table 4-4 depicts the increased value of outstanding GNMA securities that have experienced a rapid payoff rate as compared with the FHA historical data in Table 4-1.

---

[6] See Foreword in Publication No. 715, Financial Publishing Company, 82 Brookline Avenue, Boston, Massachusetts 02215.

Table 4-2
Simulated amortization of a GNMA 8 with
a 7.5 percent annual prepayment rate

GNMA coupon	Assumed prepayment rate
8%	7.5%*

Average life (years)	
Half-life	Principal weighted
7.8	9.8

Years since GNMA issued	Remaining principal balance
1	92.5%
2	85.6
3	79.2
4	73.3
5	67.8
6	62.7
7	58.0
8	53.7
9	49.7
10	45.9

*This rate was computed in Michael Waldman, *Average Life of Mortgage Related Instruments* (New York: Salomon Brothers, December 1977). It is 135 percent of normal FHA experience.

Table 4-3
FHA and GNMA mortgage mortality experience

	Average life (years)			
	Half-life		Principal weighted	
Mortgage coupon	FHA	GNMA	FHA	GNMA
6.5		11.5		12.7
7	10.8	8.8	12.3	10.6
7.5	11.0	8.2	12.4	10.0
8	11.2	7.8	12.6	9.8
8.5	11.2		12.7	

Source: Michael Waldman, *Average Life of Mortgage Related Instruments* (New York: Salomon Brothers, December 1977).

Table 4-4
GNMA price analysis based on payoff rate

Payoff rate of average FHA experience	Price of newly issued GNMA 9's at specified GNMA yield levels				
	8.00%	8.50%	9.00%	9.50%	10.00%
100%.....	106.77	103.10	99.63	96.36	93.27
150......	105.93	102.70	99.63	96.71	93.94
200......	105.27	102.39	99.63	97.00	94.48
250......	104.80	102.16	99.63	97.20	94.87
300......	104.33	101.94	99.63	97.41	95.27

Source: *Pass-Through Yield and Value Tables,* Publication No. 715 (Boston: Financial Publishing Company).

PRICING GNMA CASH FORWARD MARKET SECURITIES

The pricing techniques reviewed above have greatly improved the ability of an analyst to determine the proper value of a GNMA security that is available for immediate delivery. Once its nearby price has been validated, traders must also be able to compute the appropriate prices for deferred transactions, since the security is actively traded in forward months.

In the typical commodity storage charge market for corn, prices for the more distant months of the same crop tend to be higher than prices for nearby months. Therefore a trader can buy a nearby contract and sell the deferred contract. Delivery of the commodity can be taken in the nearby month and held for redelivery against the short position in the deferred month. This kind of arbitrage tends to keep the deferred contract price from rising above the nearby contract price by more than the cost of storage between the two contract months. Obviously, this is only an approximation. Other market factors, including expectations, play an important role in creating fluctuations in spreads between contract months.

In the GNMA market this relationship is inverted. Prices generally tend to decline from the nearby to the deferred contract. This relationship may be thought of as a negative storage charge and is referred to as *backwardation*. It occurs when long-term interest rates are higher than short-term rates. The greater the breakage (difference) between long- and short-term rates, the greater is the profit of ownership. This relationship was reversed from the fourth quarter of 1973 to the first quarter of 1974, and again beginning September 1978 until April 1979. This reversal caused the future months' prices to be equal to or more expensive than the price of the nearby security.

An investor who owns a GNMA certificate during normal times can borrow against it by pledging it as collateral and still earn income. Security dealers call this strategy a *reverse repo* transaction. It is usually limited to government securities. The income of the security holder is related to the GNMA security coupon rate, while the expense to finance the security is tied to broker, commercial paper, and prime rates.

Assume a pension fund purchases a GNMA 8 at par, and then repos the security through a GNMA dealer at 6.7 percent for 30 days. The fund's net income per $1 million for a 30-day reverse repo period is computed in the following way:

Step 1:   Annual interest income = $80,000
Step 2:   Annual interest expense = $67,000
Step 3:   Annual interest breakage = $13,000

Step 4: $$\frac{\$13,000 \times 30 \text{ days}}{360 \text{ days/year}} = \$1,083 \text{ monthly income}$$

If the short-term borrowing rate is 5 percent as it was during the summer of 1977, the same transaction results in a profit of $2,499 per month.

Return on investment is another way to compute profitability. Since a GNMA dealer or a repo lender provides the pension fund between 99 and 97 cents on the dollar for a 30-day repo, the fund has an approximate return of 4 to 11 percent per month on its investment.[7] If the equity value of the GNMA security can be maintained or increased during this same period of time, it becomes

---

[7] See Marcia Stigum, *The Money Market: Myth, Reality, and Practice* (Homewood, Ill.: Dow Jones-Irwin, 1978), chap. 12.

even more attractive. Another way of stating this observation is: the steeper the yield curve, the more profitable is the transaction, regardless of the prevailing rate level.[8]

Table 4-5 can be used to determine the approximate monthly profits from a one-month reverse repo transaction for a $1 million GNMA 8 purchased at par, which is pledged as collateral for a 99 percent loan against its face value.

Table 4-5
Monthly income from GNMA repo transaction

Interest rate differential between GNMA coupon and short-term borrowing rate (basis points)	Dollars	Monthly repo profit per $1 million (1/64's)
50	416	2.6
75	624	3.9
100	833	5.3
125	1,041	6.7
150	1,250	8.0
200	1,666	10.7
250	2,083	13.3

It is now simple to determine the theoretical price of a GNMA security that is available for settlement in 30, 60, or 90 days when its immediate or nearby price is known. If the breakage between long- and short-term rates is 200 BP, refer to Table 4-5 and divide the income generated from this repo transaction by $312.50.[9] In this example, $1,666 ÷ $312.50 = 5.3. Therefore, if immediate GNMA 8's are priced at 98-16, a GNMA 8 that is to be delivered in 30 days should command a price of 98-10 or 98-11. This calculation illustrates the effect of backwardation.

Another approach in determining the pricing of back months is to understand a mortgage originator's profit plan. Normally, a mortgage banker originates FHA/VA loans at a discount. This technique is used to originate FHA mortgages at yields that are equiva-

---

[8] Historical curves relating current yields to maturities for Treasury bills, notes, and bonds are depicted in Table 10-2.
[9] A price change of 1/32 for a $1 million GNMA security is worth $312.50.

lent to the current market. If the FHA mortgage contract rate is 8.5 percent and the secondary FHA market rate is 8.75 percent, a mortgage originator must originate loans at an 1.25-point discount to break even. Therefore, the mortgage banker pays $34,562 for an 8.5 percent FHA mortgage with a balance of $35,000. The loan is then warehoused with a commercial bank at or near prime, or financed by selling commercial paper.[10] When it is sold and delivered to a permanent investor, the short-term obligation is retired.

The mathematics of a warehousing transaction that takes place on December 15, 1977, is as follows:

Warehousing income
    mortgage rate 8.5 percent
Average cost of inventory warehoused
    98.75 percent of par
Warehousing expense
    cost of funds 7.25 percent
Other expenses
    servicing loans while in warehouse 0.25 percent

Monthly warehousing profit and loss study for $1 million

$$\text{Warehousing profit} = \text{Income} - \text{Expenses}$$

$$\text{Income} = \frac{\text{Mortgage balance} \times \text{Mortgage rate}}{12}$$

$$\text{Expense} = \frac{\text{Acquisition cost} \times \text{Short-term borrowing cost} \times \text{Percent loaned}}{12} + \frac{\text{Mortgage balance} \times \text{Servicing rate}}{12}$$

$$\text{Monthly profit} = \frac{\$1,000,000 \times 0.085}{12} - \left[\frac{(987,500)(0.0725)(0.97)}{12} + \frac{\$1,000,000 \times 0.0025}{12} \right]$$

$$= \$7,083 - (\$5,787 + \$208) = \$1,088$$

These figures demonstrate that the mortgage banker earns $1,088 per month for every $1 million of loans being warehoused. The banker can break even if these loans are sold 30 days later for 7/64 less than the immediate price. In this example, this number

---

[10] Warehousing is a commercial banking function that temporarily finances closed mortgages at short-term rates.

53

becomes the monthly backwardation or convergence variable based on existing yield spreads of long- minus short-term rates.

On December 15, 1977, the actual bid spread for a GNMA 8 between December 1977 and January 1978 was 5/32 in the GNMA cash forward market. This calculation confirms that the spreads that day were reasonable.

A precise correlation between the GNMA cash market and a warehousing function is difficult to measure, since few mortgage companies have the availability of short-term funds at the most efficient levels. When spreads vary from these mathematical relationships, it is usually a function of expectations or a momentary demand for a specific GNMA coupon.

Until now only the mathematical relationships that affect pricing have been reviewed. Some attention must be given to the psychology of the money market, as money managers have the knack of becoming self-prophesizing.

When examining back month prices, both the mathematical relationships and the psychic or predictive function should be considered. If, in January 1978, the price in the cash forward market for March GNMA 8's is 96-16 and the price for September 8's is 95-20, then the six-month spread is 28/32. If the mathematical spread relationship calls for a 20/32 spread, the additional 8/32 must be related to the psychic barrier. The trading community is probably projecting a steeper yield curve during the second half of 1978. If the contracts were trading only 16/32 apart, the inverse assumption must be made.

Now that the pricing of a GNMA security in the immediate and forward market has been reviewed, let us analyze how the nearby GNMA mortgage interest rate futures contract should be priced.

PRICING GNMA MORTGAGE INTEREST RATE FUTURES CONTRACTS

Currently there are three GNMA mortgage interest rate contracts traded on two regulated U.S. exchanges. The primary difference among the contracts revolves about their contractual delivery system. These are thoroughly reviewed in Chapter 7.

Name of GNMA futures contracts	Exchange	Date of first trade
Collateralized depository receipt	CBOT	October 20, 1975
Certificate delivery contract	CBOT	September 13, 1978
Certificate delivery contract	ACE	September 12, 1978

Since the collateralized depository receipt (CDR) contract is the oldest and most active one, the pricing techniques defined in this section are tailored to that contract. However, the procedures described in pricing a CDR contract can be used to price the other contracts. They will be simpler to compute since in most cases they prohibit the delivery of securities at prices above par. Thus it will be unnecessary to identify the cheapest eligible GNMA security for delivery, since the ACE and certificate delivery contracts are priced according to their relationships to the current GNMA production coupon.

PRICING A COLLATERALIZED DEPOSITORY RECEIPT GNMA CONTRACT

If there is any agreement among professional GNMA dealers related to trading GNMA futures contracts, it pertains to the difficulty in determining a standard pricing formula. There are numerous techniques that can be used to develop the correct theoretical price of a nearby GNMA futures contract. This simulated price should have a close correlation to the cheapest GNMA security readily available for delivery in the cash market. This chapter uses the premium bond theory to determine a reasonable futures price. If at a given moment all securities are priced at a discount, the cheapest available coupon can be substituted for the premium-priced GNMA security.

Any single-family GNMA pass-through security can be used to make a delivery against an open CDR GNMA contract provided it has an average life of 12 years, and is collateralized by a 30-year insured or guaranteed mortgage with uniform mortgage rates. On December 30, 1978, more than $65 billion of single-family GNMAs had been issued. Table 4-6 shows the remaining dollar volume of the most popular coupons as of that date.

Table 4-6
Outstanding principal balance of
GNMA securities by coupon
as of December 30, 1978

Coupon	Amount outstanding ($ millions)
6.50	$ 3,098
7	262
7.25	2,342
7.50	7,806
7.75	340
8	18,714
8.25	3,977
8.50	4,091
9	6,015

Source: Government National Mortgage Association.

All of these coupons, plus other less popular ones, could be used to satisfy a delivery. If a seller decides to deliver a depository receipt in satisfying an open position, the most economical coupon at that given moment will be selected to collateralize the depository receipt.

Calculations of equivalent principal balances

Since CDR contractual obligations require an 8 percent GNMA certificate with a principal balance of $100,000 yielding 8 percent, securities with other than 8 percent coupons require different principal balances to generate an equivalent yield. Alternative balances for purposes of delivery can be computed by the following approach:

Step 1: Determine the yield of GNMA 8's at par. GNMA yield books (Financial Publishing Company's Publication Nos. 715, 736, or 746) indicate the GNMA yield to be 7.96 percent.

56

Step 2: The equivalent principal balance of GNMAs bearing coupons other than 8 percent that are required to satisfy the delivery regulations of the CDR contract can be calculated by using the following formula:

$$\begin{array}{l}\text{Principal balance of GNMA } X \\ \text{(other than 8's) satisfactory for} \\ \text{delivery against one contract}\end{array} = (\$100,000)\left(\begin{array}{l}\text{Conversion factor} \\ \text{for GNMA } X\text{'s}\end{array}\right)$$

This formula introduces the term *conversion factor.* It is a constant associated with a GNMA coupon other than 8 percent, which when multiplied by \$100,000 produces a yield equal to \$1.00 of a GNMA 8 at par. Table 4-7 is a listing of these factors.

Table 4-7
Conversion factors for CDR GNMA mortgage
interest rate futures contract

GNMA interest (percent)	Conversion factor
6.50%	1.12123
7.00	1.07816
7.25	1.05820
7.50	1.03806
7.75	1.01867
8.00	1.00000
8.25	0.98219
8.50	0.96501
9.00	0.93167
9.50	0.900322
9.75	0.885609
10.00	0.871460

Source: *CBOT Delivery Manual.* © 1977, Chicago Board of Trade.

Thus, if J. R. Short considered delivering GNMAs to satisfy a short position, J. R. Short would perform the following steps:

Step 1: Multiply the dollar amount of the open contracts to be delivered by the conversion factors for GNMA 6.5's, 8's, and 9's as found in Table 4-7.

Coupon	Conversion factor
6.5	1.12123 X \$100,000
8	1.00000 X 100,000
9	0.93167 X 100,000

Step 2: In the GNMA offered side price quotation from *The Wall Street Journal,* the following closing price was listed for the evening of December 14, 1977:

Coupon	Price	Yield
6.5	$88^{28}\!/_{32}$	7.99
8	$97^{16}\!/_{20}$	8.28
9	104%	8.36

Multiply the result of Step 1 by the dollar price of the coupons. (If they are purchased from a GNMA dealer, use the price from the offered side of the immediate market.)

Coupon	Dollar amount of face value required/contract		Offered Price		Total acquisition cost/contract
6.5	$112,123.30	X	89.00	=	$99,789
8	100,000.00	X	97.625	=	97,625
9	93,167.70	X	104.250	=	97,127

Step 3: Step 2 determines the most economical delivery cost. Judging from these results, J. R. Short would undoubtedly purchase GNMA 9's on December 14. This cost relationship can vary daily, but if a premium-priced bond exists it will generally be the least expensive to purchase.

Since premium-priced bonds are almost always ineligible for delivery against an ACE or certificate delivery GNMA contract on the CBOT, premium priced bonds can be omitted in computing delivery costs for those contracts. It is satisfactory to compute optimal cost levels based on the immediate cash price of a current coupon.

PRICING A NEARBY CDR GNMA FUTURES CONTRACT

To determine if the price level of the nearby CDR contract is reasonable, an Immediate Value Test (I.V.T.) is performed. This procedure compares the nearby CDR GNMA futures price to the immediate cash market price of the cheapest available GNMA security. In order to equate both markets the effects of convergence must be included, where appropriate.

The following steps must be completed:

Step 1: Record least expensive GNMA offered price from *The Wall Street Journal.*

Step 2: Convert 1/32 to decimals.

Step 3: Multiply result from Step 2 by conversion factor associated with cheapest coupon.

Step 4: Convert result developed in Step 3 to 1/32's. This is called the equivalent price. It can be compared to the current nearby price of the CDR contract. If the 8's equivalent price is greater than the CDR GNMA contract price, the contract is cheap and is ideal for buying. If the equivalent price is lower than the GNMA contract price, the CDR GNMA futures contract is suitable for shorting.

Step 5: If the nearby month is not the same as the immediate cash market month, the 8's equivalent price must be adjusted for backwardation before it is compared to the CDR GNMA futures price. When the yield curve is normal the equivalent price must be decreased to reflect carrying profits as described in Table 4-5. When the yield curve is inverted, the equivalent price may have to be increased to reflect the cost to carry.

To test this procedure, let us use the December 14, 1977, prices referred to in the Equivalent Balance section.

Step 1: 104-08

Step 2: 104.25

Step 3: $104.06 \times 0.931 = 97.056$

Step 4: 97-02

Step 5: Not applicable since the nearby futures contract month is also December.

Step 6: 97-02 is the 8's equivalent price,
The December 14, 1977 CDR GNMA future price was 97-04 at the close of business.

Conclusion: Contract is neutrally priced but favors a short position.

An additional example of this technique uses data from February 14, 1977. During this period the government bond market was under significant downward pressure.

Step 1:   105-24
Step 2:   105.75
Step 3:   105.75 × 0.931 = 98.45
Step 4:   98-14
Step 5:   Subtract 8/32 from 8's equivalent price to reflect current interest rate levels for one month.
Step 6:   98-06 is the 8's equivalent price,
            97-27 is the March CDR GNMA closing price on February 14, 1977.

Conclusion: Contract is underpriced and favors a long position.

Therefore, if an investor wishes to take a short position on February 14, the March 1977 contract should be avoided. This contract is already oversold.

An alternative procedure for determining whether a contract is favorably priced for a long or short position is to develop a histori-

Table 4-8
Basis study between immediate GNMA cash market* and nearby CDR futures contract

Date	Immediate GNMA cash price		Nearby CDR futures price	Basis (in 1/32)	
	7.5's	8's		7.5's	8's
6/01/77	95-26	99-09	98-29	− 99	12
7/01/77	96-23	100-04	98-30	− 71	38
8/01/77	95-22	99-07	98-23	− 99	13
9/01/77	96-06	99-13	98-29	− 87	16
10/04/77	95-26	98-29	97-26	− 64	35
11/01/77	94-10	97-24	97-01	− 87	23
12/02/77	94-18	97-12	96-16	− 90	16
1/04/78	93-00	96-16	95-20	− 84	28
2/01/78	91-29	95-10	94-18	− 85	24
3/01/78	92-20	94-30	94-27	−103	3
4/03/78		94-19	93-13		38
5/01/78		94-02	93-12		22
6/01/78		92-15	92-00		15
7/01/78		91-15	90-00		47
8/01/78		92-13	91-19		26
9/01/78		93-10	92-24		18

*Bid quotation.

60

cal record that tracks the immediate cash market bid price for a GNMA security and the closing price of the nearby contract. If both prices are recorded at approximately 3:15 EDT a comparison can be made on the basis relationships over a period of time. Using 3:15 EDT is suggested because the cash market continues to trade until 4:30 EDT. If one is unaware of this time discrepancy, it is possible to discover significant distortions when using *The Wall Street Journal's* GNMA cash quotations to analyze comparative futures price movements. Table 4-8 is an example of such a ledger. It tracks GNMA 7.5's and 8's and develops a factor that is the basis between the immediate cash price and the price of a selected futures contract month. After adjusting the factor for backwardation, it is relatively simple to obtain a preliminary indication of the futures contract price level.

Convergence

The nearby CDR futures contract can be expected to trade at the GNMA cash spot price during its last day of trading. Since the contract is tracking the cheapest coupon, it cannot always be bought or sold at the price of a discount bond. On December 2, 1977, the premium-priced GNMA 9's traded at a yield of 8.27 and the discounted GNMA 8's traded at 8.22. Since one basis point is worth approximately 5/64, it can be estimated that the December futures price should go off the board about 25/64 or 12/32 below the cash 8's price, if the spread between the cash market GNMA 8's and 9's remains intact until the expiration date of the futures contract.

The basis between the prices of discount and premium Treasury bonds varies widely.[11] It is a function of current market yield levels and the yield curve. The lower the current yield level for long-maturity bonds, the greater is the yield spread between discount and premium Treasury bonds. On December 15, 1976, the yield spread between GNMA 8's and 9's in the cash market was 19 BP. The yield level at that time was 7.63 for GNMA 8

---

[11] See Sidney Homer and Martin Leibowitz, *Inside the Yield Book* (Englewood Cliffs, N.J.: Prentice-Hall, 1973).

pass-through securities. On April 22, 1978, this yield spread was flat. GNMAs were then trading at a yield of 8.73. Table 4-9 illustrates the basis relationships on the last day of trading for GNMA futures contracts that expired during 1977 and 1978.

The liquidity of the back contract months should also be examined to determine whether the last trades could have temporarily

Table 4-9
Basis relationship between immediate cash market GNMA 8's and nearby
CDR futures contracts on expiration date of contract

Last day of trade	Cash 8's price	GNMA yield	Nearby CDR futures contract	Futures yield*	Cash over futures (1/32)
3/22/77	98-14	8.17	98-08	8.19	6
6/21/77	99-30	7.96	99-16	8.02	14
9/21/77	99-10	8.04	98-24	8.12	18
12/20/77	96-26	8.39	96-14	8.45	12
3/21/78	95-20	8.58	95-25	8.54	−5
6/21/78	92-00	9.10	91-22	9.15	10
9/20/78	92-22	9.00	92-16	9.02	6
12/19/78	89-30	9.42	88-01	9.72	61†

*This yield generally represents the cheapest available GNMA coupon on the expiration date.
†GNMA 8's were very expensive at this time.

overstated or understated their values. This could occur if the liquidity in the back months was thin. On December 20, 1977, the CDR GNMA open contracts were as shown below.

These figures indicate a relatively even distribution with the exception of December 1977, which was to cease trading in two days. It

Month	Open interest
December 1977	224
March 1978	2,562
June 1978	1,956
September 1978	2,630
December 1978	3,489
March 1979	2,942
June 1979	2,950
September 1979	1,629
Total	19,886

is noteworthy that most December 1977 contracts evidently had already been offset during the previous weeks and few deliveries could be expected. This is in agreement with normal expectations.

To resume the pricing evaluation of the GNMA futures contracts, on December 20, 1977, we find that the December 1977 GNMA futures were priced at 96-30 and the bid side of the cash market for immediate GNMA 8's was 97-12. The basis was 14/32 off the bid side. On December 20, 1977, *The Wall Street Journal* indicated a yield differential between GNMA 8's and 9's in the immediate cash market of 7 BP. Since the GNMA 9's were premium bonds, they were probably cheaper than GNMA 8's. Using a rule of thumb that 5/64 approximates 1 BP for a GNMA security, the December GNMA futures contracts should be priced at 17/32 below cash GNMA 8's on their last day of trading. Subtracting 17/32 from the cash GNMA 8 price of 97-12 results in a remainder of 96-27. The assumption can now be made that December was fairly priced at 96-30. Coincidentally this price was verified by an I.V.T. procedure.

A second approach to testing the price levels of back month contracts is based on analyzing the income generated from lending long and borrowing short. On December 20, 1977, GNMA 8's were yielding 8.30 percent and short-term funds could be borrowed at 6.60 percent for 30 days. From Table 4-5, it is determined that the monthly profit will be $1,417 per $1 million. This converts to 9/64 per month, if $1,417 is divided by $312.50. Therefore, each contract should be trading at 13/32 or 14/32 below the previous one, since they are trading three months apart.

Upon reexamination, we find the following spread relationships in existence on December 20, 1977.

Month	Price	Month	Price	Difference
December 1977	96-30	March 1978	96-11	19/32
March 1978	96-11	June 1978	95-28	15/32
June 1978	95-28	September 1978	95-18	10/32
September 1978	95-18	December 1978	95-09	9/32
December 1978	95-09	March 1979	95-01	8/32
March 1979	95-01	June 1979	94-27	6/32
June 1979	94-27	September 1979	94-18	9/32

The following conclusions can be drawn from these quotations. The basis relationship for the nearby month is in an acceptable range based on an IVT. March 1978 is probably cheap, since December 1977 will go off the board in two days. If there were a requirement for a long hedge, for a short time March 1978 should be selected. If a short position were desired, June 1978 is preferable to the back months if expectations continue for a flattening yield curve.

In selecting the proper contract for positioning a hedge, future yield curve expectations should be incorporated into the decision process. If the curve is expected to flatten appreciably, a front month should be selected for a short position and a back month for taking a long position. Similarly, if the yield curve is expected to widen, there should be a short position in a back month and a long position in a nearby contract.

PRICING THE LONG–TERM U.S. TREASURY BOND CONTRACT

Long-term U.S. Treasury bonds have no forward market similar to that in GNMAs. They are usually traded for cash, overnight, or five-day settlement. Therefore, the U.S. Treasury bond futures contract can be priced only from the immediate market. The contract provides for delivery of $100,000 principal of any issue of contract-grade bonds. This latter classification is defined completely in Chapter 7.

The only pertinent characteristic useful for pricing pertains to the 15-year remaining life. All eligible issues are priced to yield 8 percent at par. To assist a trader in computing an equivalent price for securities with other than 8 percent coupons, the Financial Publishing Company publishes a special brochure, No. 765. It lists the conversion factors necessary to compute the amount a short seller of a U.S. Treasury bond futures contract can bill the long buyer when a delivery occurs. To obtain an invoice amount, this factor is multiplied by the U.S. Treasury contract price that is in existence on the settlement date.

In March 1978 the Treasury bond outstanding with the longest maturity was the Treasury 7⅞ of 11/15/07/02. Its remaining life was 24 years and six months, since it is callable in 2002. If a March 1978 U.S. Treasury contract was sold at 94-08, the short would invoice the long $92,996 if he or she chose to deliver the Treasury 7⅞ of 2002. This is computed in the following manner:

Step 1: Factor for 7⅞ percent bond with remaining life of 24 years and six months is 0.9867.

Step 2: Notice day settlement price (assumed) is 94-08, or decimal equivalent 94.25.

Step 3:
$$
\begin{array}{r}
0.9425 \\
\times\ 0.9867 \\
\hline
0.92996
\end{array}
$$

Step 4:
$$
\begin{array}{rl}
0.92996 & \\
\times\ \$100,000 & \text{contract amount} \\
\hline
\$\ 92,996 & \text{invoice amount}
\end{array}
$$

Therefore, the immediate U.S. Treasury bond futures price is related to the cheapest eligible Treasury bond that can be purchased or sold in the cash market. This is normally the security with the longest remaining maturity beyond 15 years.

On March 1979 long-term U.S. Treasury bonds were deliverable in the CBOT futures contract as shown in Table 4-10.

Table 4-10
Long-term U.S. Treasury bonds deliverable in the CBOT T-bond
futures contract as of 3/30/79

Coupon	Maturity	Maturity terms	December delivery conversion factor	Outstanding amount ($ billions)
3	1995	15-2	0.5603	$ 0.5
3½	1998	19-1	0.5617	1.9
7⅞	1995-00	15-2	0.9890	2.8
8⅜	1995-00	16-0	1.0335	4.7
8	1996-01	17-0	1.0000	1.6
8¼	2000-05	20-3	1.0249	4.2
7⅝	2002-07	22-2	0.9611	4.2
7⅞	2002-07	23-1	0.9867	1.5
8⅜	2003-08	24-0	1.0397	2.1
8¾	2003-08	24-1	1.0795	5.2
			Total	$28.7

Source: CBOT Interest Rate Futures Newsletter, March 3, 1979. © 1979, Chicago Board of Trade.

Forward months should be priced according to the same principles used to evaluate GNMA forward prices. Spreads should be a function of carrying costs as reflected by possible repo and reverse repo transactions. Normally spreads narrow as the yield curve flattens and widen when the yield curve widens. This makes a price inversion possible when the yield curve is flat or inverted. Long-term U.S. Treasury futures contracts should be continually compared with similar GNMA interest rate futures contracts for price trends and relative performance. Figure 4-4 is an example of this basis relationship between the nearby contracts.

PRICING T-BILL CONTRACTS

On December 31, 1978, there were two T-bill contracts trading on the Chicago Mercantile Exchange. The oldest and best known is a 90-day T-bill contract, which began trading in January 1976. The one-year T-bill contract was posted 30 months later.

Pricing these instruments is far simpler than computing the price levels for GNMA and long-term U.S. Treasury bond contracts. The T-bill contract is priced in relationship to the 90-day T-bill. It has liquidity and is understood by all members of the financial community. The quality of T-bills is uniform; their only variation is maturity.

T-bills are sold every Monday by the Federal Reserve at an auction. They are sold on a discount basis, below their face value, and are redeemed on maturity at par. The difference represents interest. On December 18, 1978, three-month T-bills were sold at a price of 97.668. Buyers had to put up $976,668 per $1 million. The difference, $23,332, is divided by the face amount of $1 million to obtain an interest rate of 2.33 percent for the 91-day period. To convert this percentage to the customary annual yield, the 2.33 percent is divided by 91 days and multiplied by 360 days. This produces an annual discount rate of 9.23 percent for the 91-day T-bill.

Until recently the only place to purchase a T-bill was in the cash market. Now a new market is available to the investor and trader—

Figure 4-4
Price relationship between nearby GNMA and long-term U.S. Treasury
bond futures contracts, October 1977 to July 1978

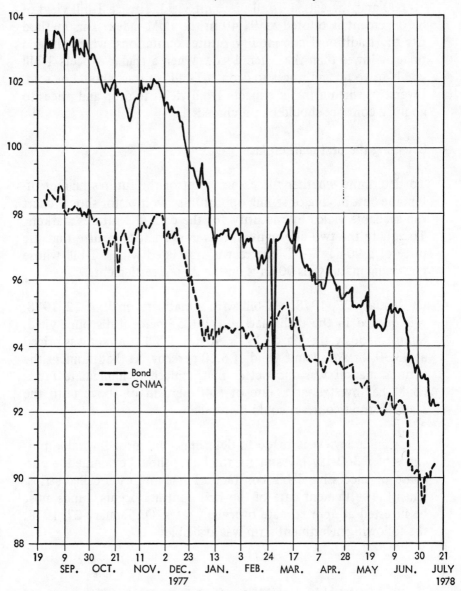

Source: Telerate Historical Data Base, Rapidata, Inc.

67

the futures market. T-bill contracts are quoted in terms of an International Monetary Market (IMM) price index. The IMM system is essentially an index based on the difference between 100.00 and the actual T-bill discount yield. Thus, a T-bill yield of 8.60 percent is quoted as 91.40 in the IMM index. This method fits the traditional commodity futures quotations, where the bid price is lower than the offered side. When a trader expects T-bill yields to go up and prices to drop, a T-bill contract should be sold. Inversely, when a trader expects T-bill yields to drop and prices to go up, a contract should be purchased.

Selecting the best marketplace

To determine whether the cash market or the futures market offers the best buying or selling opportunity an investor should chart the available yields by maturity for the cash and futures markets. To equate the two alternatives, it is important to realize that the price of a 90-day T-bill contract is associated with a T-bill whose remaining maturity is 90 days on the day of settlement.

On January 27, 1978, a T-bill with a maturity on June 22, 1978, was quoted in the cash market at a 6.55 percent discount yield. Simultaneously the March 1978, 90-day T-bill contract was priced at 93.30, or a discount yield of 6.70 percent. At that moment the futures market was the better marketplace if immediate funds could be invested at a rate of 6.40 percent or above until the March futures contract could be funded.

If a similar review is made to determine the most favorable purchase of a 360-day investment, the buyer should examine the purchase of successive T-bill contracts. These are often called strips. Until the settlement date of the first contract occurs, funds must be invested at approximate overnight rates. On January 27, 1978, the following investment strip was available:

	Discount rate
Overnight funds, 1/27/78 to 3/23/78	6.75%
March 1978, 90-day T-bill contract	6.70
June 1978, 90-day T-bill contract	7.13
September 1978, 90-day T-bill contract	7.43
Average for 12-month investment	7.00%

This average should be compared with an immediate purchase of a T-bill maturing on December 12, 1978, at 6.78 percent. It is obvious that on January 27, 1978, the one-year investment strip was superior.

Similar pricing techniques can be used to determine the price level of the one-year T-bill contract. A strip of one-year contracts can become an alternative to purchasing a note with a remaining maturity of two or three years. These contracts can also be used to secure available yield levels for future investments when cash is not immediately available.

As of December 1978, T-bill contracts are the only liquid interest rate futures contracts suitable for extensive money market cross hedging. Figure 4-5 depicts the relative yield relationships of 90-day T-bill discount yields to federal funds and the Federal Reserve discount rate.

In summary, pricing T-bill futures contracts is relatively simple. When the basis between forward months and the yield curve becomes abnormal, there is a trading opportunity for either a buy or sell. It can be executed quickly and inexpensively by professional hedgers and speculators.

PRICING COMMERCIAL PAPER

These contracts are priced similarly to T-bill contracts. Contracts are priced on a discount yield basis but are displayed in terms of yield. A quotation of 11.50 percent is identical with quotes in the money markets in which 90-day commercial paper is traded.

All orders should be placed at a specific price. Market orders should be avoided. Contract prices generally reflect the cheapest 90-day paper rated A-1 by Standard & Poor's Corporation or P-1 by Moody's Investors Service. Check with your representative to determine which specific issues are currently approved by the CBOT for delivery.

Figure 4-6 depicts the yield relationship between the nearby commercial paper contract and a consensus prime rate. It becomes

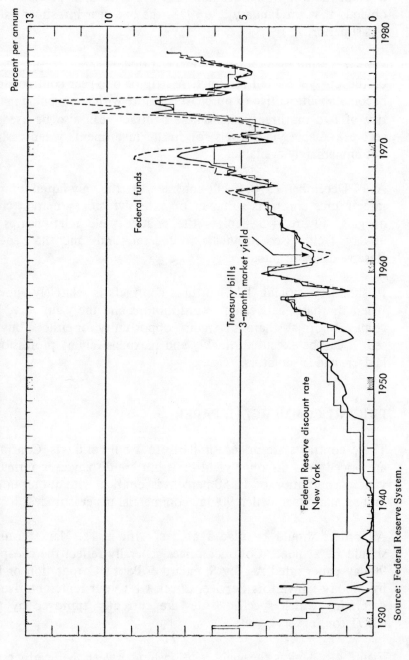

Figure 4-5

Yield relationships between 90-day T-bills and Federal Reserve discount rate and federal funds (short-term interest rates)

Percent per annum

Federal funds

Treasury bills
3-month market yield

Federal Reserve discount rate
New York

Source: Federal Reserve System.

apparent that spreads narrow significantly as demand increases for short-term commercial financing.

In conclusion, commercial paper contracts should be watched and charted closely. When their liquidity improves, they make an excellent vehicle for cross hedging short-term borrowing costs tied to prime, certificates of deposit, or banker's acceptance paper.

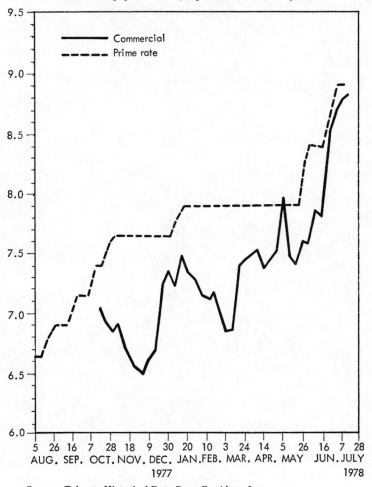

Figure 4-6
Yield relationship between concensus prime rate and nearby 90-day commercial paper contract, September 1977 to July 1978

Source: Telerate Historical Data Base, Rapidata, Inc.

How to read a yield book

UNDERSTANDING THE YIELD BOOK

Learning to interpret a yield manual is imperative for anyone who trades bonds and interest rate futures contracts. The yield book is the common denominator for thousands of fixed income securities, each with unique characteristics. To manually equate in value a 5 percent coupon to a 3 percent coupon, or a 10-year maturity to a 12-year maturity, is difficult and most assuredly impractical. The most frequently used yield books are published by the Financial Publishing Company of Boston. These publications are tailored to the specific needs of the user. In this book, the publications in the following table have been referenced frequently.

Name of publication	Publication number
Expanded Bond Values Tables	83
Pass-Through Yield and Value Tables for GNMA Mortgage-Backed Securities	715
Net Yield Table for GNMA Mortgage-Backed Securities	710
Financial-GNMA Yield and Price Equivalent Tables	736
Treasury Bond Futures Conversion Factors	765
Mortgage Participation Yield Book	770

Publication No. 83 is used most often. This manual lists prices for securities that pay interest semiannually until maturity. (See Figure 5-1 for a sample page.) It is divided into sections by coupons. The coupon rates are printed in the upper corners of the pages. Across the top of each page are headings identifying the remaining years and months to maturity for any selected coupon. The far left vertical column is a listing of yields in ascending order. To find the price of a specific security, one need only turn to the appropriate coupon and select the proper remaining maturity column. Since the yield is known, simply locate the yield in the left-hand column and read across to the selected maturity column. The appropriate price is the intersection. Yields can be determined in the reverse manner.

Determining the yield for a discount bond[1]

The approximate yield to maturity of a discount bond is computed in the following way:

Step 1: Compute the profit earned over the remaining life of the bond by subtracting the acquisition price from its maturity value. (This is usually its par value.)

Step 2: Divide this amount by the remaining years outstanding.

Step 3: Add the above amount to the annual interest amount paid each year.

Step 4: Divide the result from Step 3 by the average of the maturity price and the acquisition price.

The yield to maturity for a 6 percent bond maturing in five years and selling at $800 can be computed in the following manner:

Step 1: $1,000 − $800 = $200

Step 2: $200/5 = $40 per year

Step 3: 0.06% × $1,000 = $60 interest per year
$60 + $40 = $100

Step 4: $100/[($1,000 + $800)/2] = $100/$900 = 11%

Since this is only an approximation, a yield book must be used for precision. In addition, a price may be determined on numerous

---

[1] See Sidney Homer and Martin Leibowitz, *Inside the Yield Book* (Englewood Cliffs, N.J.: Prentice-Hall, 1963), chap. 1.

YEARS and MONTHS   8%

Yield	4-9	4-10	4-11	5-0	5-3	5-6	5-9	6-0
4.00	117.14	117.41	117.69	117.97	118.76	119.57	120.36	121.15
4.20	116.20	116.46	116.72	116.98	117.73	118.49	119.22	119.97
4.40	115.27	115.51	115.76	116.00	116.70	117.42	118.10	118.80
4.60	114.35	114.58	114.80	115.03	115.69	116.36	117.00	117.65
4.80	113.44	113.65	113.86	114.08	114.68	115.31	115.90	116.51
5.00	112.53	112.73	112.93	113.13	113.69	114.27	114.82	115.39
5.20	111.64	111.82	112.00	112.19	112.71	113.25	113.75	114.27
5.40	110.75	110.92	111.09	111.26	111.74	112.23	112.69	113.18
5.60	109.88	110.03	110.18	110.34	110.77	111.23	111.65	112.09
5.80	109.01	109.15	109.29	109.43	109.82	110.23	110.61	111.02
6.00	108.15	108.27	108.40	108.53	108.88	109.25	109.59	109.95
6.10	107.72	107.84	107.96	108.08	108.41	108.77	109.08	109.43
6.20	107.29	107.41	107.52	107.64	107.95	108.28	108.58	108.91
6.30	106.87	106.98	107.08	107.20	107.48	107.80	108.08	108.39
6.40	106.45	106.55	106.65	106.76	107.02	107.32	107.58	107.87
6.50	106.03	106.12	106.22	106.32	106.57	106.84	107.09	107.36
6.60	105.61	105.70	105.79	105.88	106.11	106.37	106.59	106.84
6.70	105.20	105.28	105.36	105.45	105.66	105.90	106.10	106.34
6.80	104.79	104.86	104.94	105.02	105.21	105.43	105.62	105.83
6.90	104.37	104.44	104.51	104.59	104.76	104.96	105.13	105.33
7.00	103.97	104.03	104.09	104.16	104.31	104.50	104.65	104.83
7.10	103.56	103.61	103.67	103.73	103.87	104.04	104.17	104.34
7.20	103.15	103.20	103.25	103.31	103.43	103.58	103.70	103.84
7.30	102.75	102.79	102.84	102.89	102.99	103.12	103.22	103.35
7.40	102.35	102.39	102.43	102.47	102.55	102.67	102.75	102.87
7.50	101.95	101.98	102.01	102.05	102.12	102.22	102.28	102.38
7.60	101.55	101.58	101.61	101.64	101.69	101.77	101.82	101.90
7.70	101.16	101.18	101.20	101.23	101.26	101.32	101.35	101.42
7.80	100.76	100.78	100.79	100.82	100.83	100.88	100.89	100.94
7.90	100.37	100.38	100.39	100.41	100.40	100.44	100.44	100.47
8.00	99.98	99.98	99.99	100.00	99.98	100.00	99.98	100.00
8.10	99.59	99.59	99.59	99.60	99.56	99.56	99.53	99.53
8.20	99.21	99.20	99.19	99.19	99.14	99.13	99.08	99.07
8.30	98.82	98.81	98.80	98.79	98.72	98.70	98.63	98.60
8.40	98.44	98.42	98.40	98.39	98.31	98.27	98.18	98.14
8.50	98.06	98.03	98.01	98.00	97.90	97.84	97.74	97.69
8.60	97.68	97.65	97.62	97.60	97.49	97.41	97.30	97.23
8.70	97.30	97.27	97.24	97.21	97.08	96.99	96.86	96.78
8.80	96.93	96.89	96.85	96.82	96.67	96.57	96.43	96.33
8.90	96.55	96.51	96.47	96.43	96.27	96.15	96.00	95.88
9.00	96.18	96.13	96.08	96.04	95.87	95.74	95.56	95.44
9.10	95.81	95.75	95.70	95.66	95.47	95.32	95.14	95.00
9.20	95.44	95.38	95.33	95.28	95.07	94.91	94.71	94.56
9.30	95.08	95.01	94.95	94.89	94.67	94.50	94.29	94.12
9.40	94.71	94.64	94.57	94.52	94.28	94.09	93.87	93.69
9.50	94.35	94.27	94.20	94.14	93.89	93.69	93.45	93.26
9.60	93.99	93.91	93.83	93.76	93.50	93.28	93.03	92.83
9.70	93.63	93.54	93.46	93.39	93.11	92.88	92.62	92.40
9.80	93.27	93.18	93.09	93.02	92.72	92.48	92.20	91.98
9.90	92.91	92.82	92.73	92.65	92.34	92.09	91.79	91.56
10.00	92.56	92.46	92.37	92.28	91.96	91.69	91.39	91.14
10.20	91.85	91.74	91.64	91.55	91.20	90.91	90.58	90.31
10.40	91.15	91.04	90.93	90.82	90.45	90.14	89.78	89.48
10.60	90.46	90.34	90.22	90.11	89.71	89.37	88.99	88.67
10.80	89.78	89.64	89.52	89.40	88.97	88.61	88.21	87.87
11.00	89.10	88.96	88.82	88.69	88.25	87.86	87.43	87.07
11.20	88.43	88.28	88.13	88.00	87.52	87.12	86.67	86.29
11.40	87.76	87.60	87.45	87.31	86.81	86.39	85.91	85.51
11.60	87.10	86.94	86.78	86.63	86.11	85.66	85.17	84.74
11.80	86.45	86.27	86.11	85.95	85.41	84.94	84.42	83.98
12.00	85.80	85.62	85.45	85.28	84.72	84.23	83.69	83.23

occasions when only the yield and maturity are known. Prices quoted in a yield book for discount bonds are computed in the following manner.

Assume C.J.S., the bond trader, invests in a 5 percent bond with a 20-year maturity to yield 8.00 percent. The price for this security quoted in the yield book is 70.31, or $703.10 per $1,000 bond.

After six months, or when the next interest payment is due, C.J.S. is entitled to a semiannual payment equal to $703.10 × 0.04 percent, or $28.12. However, the coupon received is for $25.00. This generates a "shortfall" of $3.12 when compared with the return computed on the basis of the purchase price. This shortfall must now be added to the original investment of $703.00, so the security has a new book value of $706.12. Opening the yield book again to the bond table that reflects the value for a 5 percent coupon with a 19½-year remaining maturity at an 8 percent yield level, C.J.S. finds a price of $706.20. The shortfalls are added continually to the acquisition costs and earn a yield equal to the yield levels of the original investment. View this as an automatic reinvestment of the shortfall. If this cycle is repeated every six months, the bond equity value will be 100, or par, at maturity. A detailed schedule of such calculations is illustrated in Table 5-1 for an investment in a 2.5 percent bond due in 20 years at an original yield level of 5 percent.

Determining the yield of a premium bond

Since bonds generally are redeemed at face value, or par, to the holder at maturity, it is apparent that an investor who purchases a bond for a price above 100 will not recover the full purchase price at the time of redemption. The investor must therefore reserve a portion of the semiannual income to retire the loss or premium amount.

Assume that C.J.S. purchases an 8 percent bond with a 20-year maturity yielding 7 percent at a price of 110.68, or $1,106.80 for a $1,000 bond. In this example C.J.S. receives a semiannual coupon worth $1,000 × 0.04 percent. This $40 coupon generates an

Table 5-1
Value table of a 2.5 percent noncallable 20-year bond bought at $686.22
to yield 5 percent held to maturity

Elapsed years	Annual investment income	Annual coupon income	Annual short-fall	New book value
1	$34.43	$25.00	$ 9.43	$ 695.65
2	34.90	25.00	9.90	705.55
3	35.41	25.00	10.41	715.96
4	35.93	25.00	10.93	726.89
5	36.48	25.00	11.48	738.37
6	37.07	25.00	12.07	750.44
7	37.68	25.00	12.68	763.12
8	38.32	25.00	13.32	776.44
9	38.99	25.00	13.99	790.43
10	39.70	25.00	14.70	805.13
11	40.45	25.00	15.45	820.58
12	41.22	25.00	16.22	836.80
13	42.05	25.00	17.05	853.85
14	42.92	25.00	17.92	871.77
15	43.82	25.00	18.82	890.59
16	44.77	25.00	19.77	910.36
17	45.78	25.00	20.78	931.14
18	46.83	25.00	21.83	952.97
19	47.93	25.00	22.93	975.90
20	49.10	25.00	24.10	1,000.00

Source: Expanded Bond Values, Financial Publishing Co.

8 percent yield for investors who purchase the security at par. However, C.J.S. purchases the security at 7 percent. This return can be achieved by a semiannual payment of $1,106.80 × 0.035 percent, or $38.74. The difference between the coupon amount of $40.00 and the required $38.74 can now be used to continually reduce the book value or acquisition cost. Therefore, after the first payment is received, the bond reflects a reduced book value of $1,106.80 less $1.26, or $1,105.34. The bond table for this security, with a remaining life of 19½ years, indicates a price of $110.55. If this cycle is repeated until maturity, the bond again will be priced at par.

If a premium bond is resold or called before maturity, any remaining unamortized premium amount must be written off as a loss.[2]

---

[2] See R. H. Cramer and Stephen L. Hawk, "The Consideration of Coupon Levels, Taxes, Reinvestment Rates and Maturities in the Investment Management of Financial Institutions," *Journal of Financial and Quantitative Analysis*, March 1975.

Table 5-2 is a detailed schedule illustrating an investment in a 7.5 percent bond with a 20-year maturity purchased to yield 5 percent. It depicts the diminishing value of a premium bond over time.

It is important to note that in neither calculation is the concept of interest on interest, known as compound interest, included in a yield book calculation. This concept would significantly enhance an investment calculation but will not be addressed in this book.[3]

Table 5-2
Value table of a 7.5 percent noncallable 20-year bond bought at $1,313.78
to yield 5 percent held to maturity

Elapsed years	Annual investment income	Annual coupon income	Annual overage	New book value
1	$65.57	$75.00	$ 9.43	$1,304.35
2	65.10	75.00	9.90	1,294.45
3	64.59	75.00	10.41	1,284.04
4	64.07	75.00	10.93	1,273.11
5	63.52	75.00	11.48	1,261.63
6	62.93	75.00	12.07	1,249.56
7	62.32	75.00	12.68	1,236.88
8	61.68	75.00	13.32	1,223.56
9	61.01	75.00	13.99	1,209.57
10	60.30	75.00	14.70	1,194.87
11	59.55	75.00	15.45	1,179.42
12	58.78	75.00	16.22	1,163.20
13	57.95	75.00	17.05	1,146.15
14	57.08	75.00	17.92	1,128.23
15	56.18	75.00	18.82	1,109.41
16	55.23	75.00	19.77	1,089.64
17	54.22	75.00	20.78	1,068.86
18	53.17	75.00	21.83	1,047.03
19	52.07	75.00	22.93	1,024.10
20	50.91	75.00	24.09	1,000.01

Source: Expanded Bond Values, Financial Publishing Co.

Interpreting GNMA yields

GNMA yields are computed differently than corporate and government bond yields. They are unique by virtue of their monthly payment of interest and principal. To equate a GNMA yield to a

[3] See Homer and Leibowitz, *Inside the Yield Book*, chap. 2.

corporate yield, an "add-on" of basis points must be made in accordance with the schedule shown in Table 5-3.

The addition of basis points to the GNMA yield recognizes the shortfall computation explained above. For GNMA securities the shortfall amount is added to the original investment amount on a

Table 5-3
Add-ons to equate GNMA and corporate bond yields

If GNMA yield is	Add to yield (basis points)
5.99-6.36	0.08
6.37-6.72	0.09
6.73-7.07	0.10
7.08-7.39	0.11
7.40-7.71	0.12
7.72-8.01	0.13
8.02-8.30	0.14
8.31-8.58	0.15
8.59-8.85	0.16
8.86-9.11	0.17
9.12-9.37	0.18
9.38-9.62	0.19
9.63-9.86	0.20
9.87-10.10	0.21
10.11-10.33	0.22
10.34-10.55	0.23
10.56-10.77	0.24
10.78-10.99	0.25

Source: Publication No. 710 (Boston: Financial Publishing Co.).

monthly basis, so additional interest is earned more rapidly. The higher the yield level in existence at acquisition time, the more additional income is generated from this automatic reinvestment stream.

Publication No. 715 can be used to compute yields and prices of GNMA securities that amortize more rapidly than the normal FHA experience. As discussed under The 12-Year Average Life in Chapter 4, the average principal weighted life of FHA mortgages is estimated to be 12 years. Since GNMA securities often pay off more rapidly, as illustrated in Table 5-4, they may amortize at a rate of 150 or 200 percent of FHA experience. If this payoff rate

Table 5-4

Effect of accelerated GNMA amortization rate on yield to maturity of GNMA 8's

Price	Amortization rate based on FHA mortality experience			
	100%	150%	200%	300%
91.00	9.33%	9.50%	9.67%	10.00%
93.00	9.00	9.13	9.26	9.51
95.00	8.69	8.78	8.87	9.04
97.00	8.39	8.44	8.49	8.58
99.00	8.10	8.11	8.12	8.15
101.00	7.82	7.79	7.77	7.72

Source: Publication No. 715 (Boston: Financial Publishing Co.).

continues to maturity, a GNMA security purchased at a discount will generate a greater yield to the investor. An example of this can be seen in Table 5-4, which lists the yields of a GNMA security purchased at a discount price but expiring in a shorter period of time.

Another way of expressing these variations is illustrated in Table 5-5, which shows the value of a security at a specific yield level when its mortality is both faster and slower than the normal FHA experience.

Table 5-5
Effect of accelerated GNMA amortization rate on price of a 9 percent GNMA security

Yield	Amortization rate based on FHA mortality experience				
	50%	100%	150%	200%	300%
11.00	86.03	87.58	88.80	89.77	91.21
10.50	89.12	90.35	91.31	92.07	93.20
10.00	92.40	93.27	93.94	94.48	95.27
9.50	95.90	96.36	96.71	97.00	97.41
9.00	99.63	99.63	99.63	99.63	99.63
8.50	103.62	103.10	102.70	102.39	101.94
8.00	107.88	106.77	105.93	105.27	104.33
7.50	112.45	110.68	109.34	108.30	106.82
7.00	117.35	114.83	112.94	111.48	109.41

Source: Publication No. 715 (Boston: Financial Publishing Co.).

Putting the yield book to work

If C.J.S. has a choice between purchasing a three-year or a five-year 8 percent government security at a price of 98, C.J.S. should turn to the page in the yield book for 8 percent coupons with three- and five-year maturities. Now C.J.S. becomes aware that the bond with the shorter maturity has a yield of 8.77 percent at a price of 98. The five-year bond with the same price generates a yield of 8.50 percent. Therefore, if the quality of both bonds is the same, the one with the shorter maturity is the better investment. This is true of only discount bonds.

A bond with an 8 percent coupon and nine years remaining to maturity is purchased at 105, yielding a return of 7.23 percent to maturity. If the bond is paid off more rapidly, C.J.S. will have $1.00 returned for every $1.05 invested before the planned maturity date. This reduces the investor's yield, since the premium is dissipated in a shorter period of time than originally estimated. To illustrate this effect refer back to Figure 5-1 and look at the six-year maturity column. If the 8 percent bond purchased at 105 is paid off or called after six years, it yields only 6.97 percent to maturity, instead of 7.23 percent to maturity. An 8 percent bond with a remaining life of six years and yielding 6.97 percent could have been purchased for approximately 103¾. Thus C.J.S. could have saved $12.50 for every $1,000 bond purchased, if C.J.S. had known in advance that the maturity of the bond would be only six years.

Charting concepts

Whether you are a speculator or hedger, you should be aware of a large cult of commodity traders who call themselves "chartists" or "technicians." They have a marked influence on the price movement of all commodity contracts because they respond primarily to technical signals instead of fundamental information. A few traders use these signals merely to validate judgments that they have developed primarily from fundamental information.

The basic philosophy of the chartist or technician, who embraces graphic historical data, is that history repeats itself. A chartist is more interested in the fact that a contract breaks its historical support level than in an explanation of why the support level was pierced. The technician looks for unusual volumes and breakouts rather than the report of the most recent Open Market Committee. The technician carefully notes when trading volumes and prices increase or when volumes increase while prices sag. Regardless of what technique is used, a technician or chartist accepts the theory that the current price reflects the consensus of all market participants. Adaptation of this concept as a replacement for evaluating and understanding fundamentals is not encouraged.

Rather the various trading techniques presented here are meant to introduce a philosophy of trading that is widely used by floor traders, brokers, and speculators.[1]

A fundamentalist believes in the theory of supply and demand. This individual carefully collects, segregates, and evaluates information that leads to conclusions about the values of contracts. If the decisions of a trader were based solely on fundamental information, he or she would be unable to participate in rapidly changing price movements caused by the placing or lifting of large positions. Often fundamental facts change more quickly than the revelations in news releases. A trader who relies solely on available fundamentals could be a day late and a dollar short. Thus, an ideal approach in trading financial futures is to combine the skills of a chartist with those of a fundamentalist.

Table 6-1 is a list of readily available fundamental information that is valuable to an interest rate futures trader.

The tools for charting are inexpensive and simple to use. Colored pencils, graph paper, and a ruler are the only necessities for the average journeyman chartist for data collection purposes. To compile additional information, a copy of *The Wall Street Journal, New York Times,* or *American Banker* probably suffices. A subscription to the *CBOT Market Newsletter* is also recommended. It can be obtained for a reasonable yearly subscription fee by writing to the Chicago Board of Trade.

BAR CHART

Bar charts are the most popular means of expression for technicians. They are simple to plot, practical to maintain, and easy to interpret. Generally, they are recorded daily, with a vertical line representing the daily price trading range of the contract. A small horizontal bar identifies the closing price on a particular day. When plotted continuously, the bars develop a pattern that may be analogous to a footprint. Analysts search for tracks they have

---

[1] See Richard J. Toweles, Charles V. Harlow, and Herbert L. Stone, *The Commodity Futures Game* (New York: McGraw-Hill Book Co., 1979), chap. 7.

Table 6-1
Monthly release dates for pertinent data affecting interest rate futures price movements*

Date	Report
October 20	GNP preliminary (third quarter 1978)
October 24	Durable goods (September)
October 26	Consumer prices (September)
	Real earnings (September)
October 27.	Export-import trade balance (September)
	Housing vacancies (third quarter 1978)
November 1	Construction expenditures (September)
	Manufacturers orders (September)
November 2	Produce prices (October)
November 3	Unemployment (October)
November 6	Consumer credit (September)
November 9	Retail sales (October)
November 13	FNMA auction results
November 15	Industrial production (October)
November 16	Inventories and sales (September)
November 17	Personal income (October)
	Housing starts (October)
	Output, capacity utilization (October)
November 20	Federal receipts and expenditures (third quarter 1978)
November 21	Gross national product (third quarter 1978)
	Federal Open Market Committee meeting
	Corporate profits (third quarter 1978)
November 22	Durable goods (October)
November 27	Real earnings (October)
	FNMA auction results
November 28	Consumer prices (October)
November 29	Export-import trade balance (October)
	Leading indicators (October)

*The precise release dates are slightly different for every month.

seen before. When they recognize a typical formation or trend, they arrive at trading decisions that will be executed with no additional supportive data. Figure 6-1 depicts some bar chart formations.

Chartists anxiously identify both support and resistance areas since they represent fundamental trading philosophies. If a price continues to reach an upper level without being able to break through that price range, the level becomes a contract's resistance area. If that area is penetrated on the upside, especially if supported by a large volume of trades, a significant price improvement can be expected. Similarly, if a price seems to repeatedly bounce off a price level that can be identified as a floor, the downward penetration of that area is considered a sell signal.

Figure 6-1
Basic bar chart formations

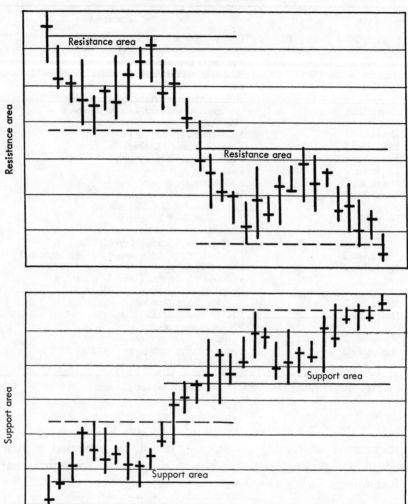

Source: *Commodity Trading Manual,* © 1977, Chicago Board of Trade.

Channels and trends

Many textbooks have been written on the subject of charting, so we will review only the most common formations. Perhaps the art of discovering channels and interpreting trends is most important. Trend lines follow straight lines and are used to estimate potential price movements.

Usually several points are required to identify and verify a trend. A clear uptrend occurs when periodic lows are made at increasing price levels. When these lows are connected for an extended time, they form a trend line. Closing prices may occur at random above the line, but none should occur below the trend line.

A downward trend is usually identified by successive daily highs that are continually lower than the previous ones.

If the lines connecting the daily lows and those connecting the daily highs are parallel, a channel has been created. Figure 6-2 is illustrative of uptrend and downtrend channels.

Channels forecast a strong technical signal for a major uptrend or downtrend. A breakout from this formation is considered very significant. It must be emphasized that forecasting trends is difficult without many observations. A chartist who responds to a small sample may often be incorrect and be whiplashed.

Head and shoulders formations

Reading footprints requires the ability to recognize patterns and formations that have been associated with specific types of animals, fowl, or humans. A similar skill is required to detect meaningful patterns in charts. The head and shoulders formation is the simplest and most important to identify.

This formation is often considered the most accurate technical barometer for predicting a reversal in the market. It consists of four distinct periods: the left shoulder, the head, the right shoulder, and an abrupt penetration of the neckline. They are depicted

Figure 6-2
Channels

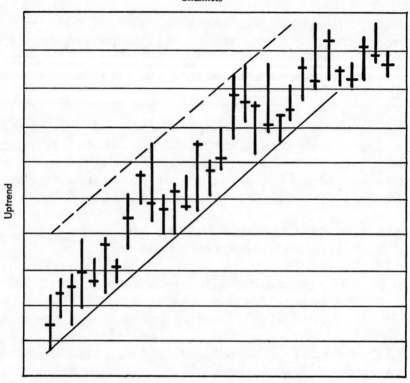

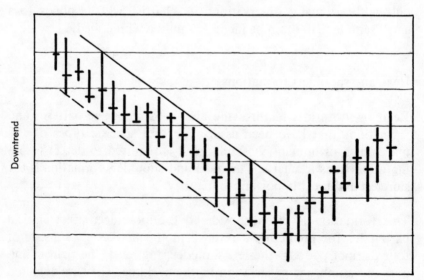

Source: *Commodity Trading Manual,* © 1977, Chicago Board of Trade.

in Figure 6-3. If the neckline is not pierced, the formation is meaningless. An inverted formation is also possible and must be considered a positive signal for a price improvement.

A common rule used to predict the possible price improvement in Figure 6-3 is that a rally should equal the distance between the top of the head and the neckline.

Figure 6-3
Head and shoulders formations

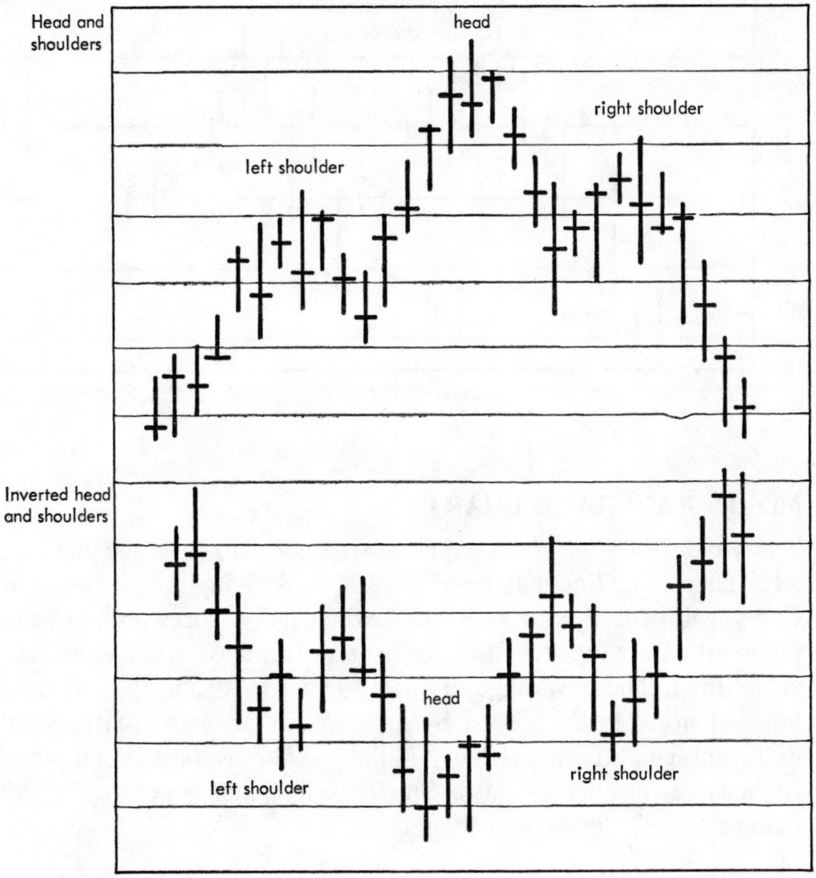

Source: *Commodity Trading Manual,* © 1977, Chicago Board of Trade.

Double tops and bottoms

Double tops and bottoms usually signal the end of a rally or trend. They are seldom perfect, and they occur within a short period of time. Frequently the second top or bottom is narrower than the first one. Figure 6-4 is illustrative of a double top.

Figure 6-4
Double tops and bottoms

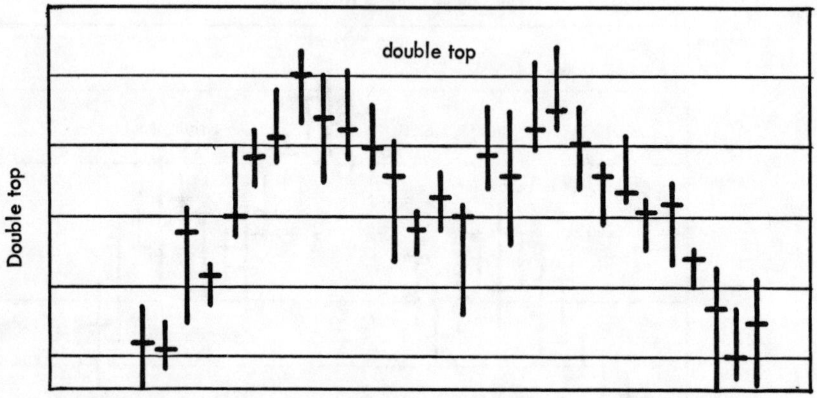

Source: *Commodity Trading Manual,* © 1977, Chicago Board of Trade.

MOVING-AVERAGE CHARTS

The moving-average chart superimposes a moving-average line over a bar chart. The line may be a 10-, 30-, or 360-day moving average. Once again, the theory states that when daily prices are above or below the moving average line, a new trend or channel will be established. The advantage of such a chart is its ability to remove unusual noise levels caused by momentary price fluctuations. Its disadvantage is its insensitivity if the moving average is computed for a large number of days. Buy or sell signals generated in this manner usually lag behind the market.

POINT-AND-FIGURE CHART

The point-and-figure chart is difficult to chart and comprehend. It is not plotted against a regular time interval but rather against changes in price movements and time. Generally, price is plotted on the vertical axis and time on the horizontal. Daily plots are not recorded at regular horizontal intervals however; rather, daily closing prices are recorded vertically until they overlap an already occupied mark. When that occurs, the plot or mark is moved to the column on the immediate right. No importance is attached to the time element. Chartists who use this approach are convinced that tracking the volume and elapsed time required to move from one price level to another is unimportant. The chart is used merely to identify the direction and potential of a price change.

To develop a point-and-figure chart, a technician must decide on a scale. The only important rule associated with a point-and-figure chart is that its scale is equal to or larger than the minimum move of the contract being charted. If we chart the long-term government contract, let us assume that a scale of 2/32 for each vertical increment has been selected.

The contract charted in Figure 6-5 began trading on Day 1 at 94-14. It closed at 94-16 on the next day, and 94-20 on the third

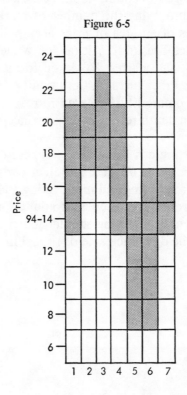

Figure 6-5

day. This last price move required two X's; one on top of the other on the same vertical axis, since the price jumped 4/32. On the fourth day, the price for this contract closed once more at 94-20. The space associated with this price had already been occupied; therefore, the space to the right of the occupied square must be marked. On the fifth day, the price closed at 94-21. Since the scale for this chart requires a 2/32 price move, no action was required. The following closing prices were recorded:

Day			Day		
	1	94-14		11	94-14
	2	94-16		12	94-14
	3	94-20		13	94-10
	4	94-20		14	94-08
	5	94-21		15	94-07
	6	94-18		16	94-08
	7	94-18		17	94-10
	8	94-19		18	94-11
	9	94-22		19	94-16
	10	94-20		20	94-16

The primary advantage of this technique is to identify areas of accumulation. Formations created by this procedure have been analyzed and cataloged in countless studies. The larger the matrix, as computed by multiplying the number of marks on the vertical and horizontal axes of an area of price accumulation, the greater is its potential price breakout. Alexander Wheelan, a point-and-figure chart expert, has charted 16 classic formations. His article, "Point and Figure Procedures in Commodity Market Analysis," published by the Commodity Research Bureau of New York, provides an excellent in-depth review of these concepts.

In conclusion, charting can be used to improve our understanding of historical price movements and to detect early changes in fundamental directions. Reading and interpreting a chart is an art, not a science. When properly utilized in conjunction with the study of related fundamentals, charting should improve the outcome of a trader's score in the dynamic game of probabilities.

Chapter 7

Making and taking delivery on interest rate futures contracts

PHILOSOPHY OF DELIVERY

Commodity markets have been repeatedly described as "not for delivery markets" by both traders and speculators. However, it is the very threat of delivery that regulates the price behavior of the futures contracts, especially during the final days of trading of the nearby contracts. Often on the last day of trading, the cash and futures markets have a perfect price relationship for identical securities. This implies that the difference between two price levels can be attributed to administrative fees. For interest rate contracts, administrative fees are negligible, since transportation, warehousing, and insurance are not required.

Price deviations that occur during the life of an interest rate contract are usually corrected rapidly by security dealers who execute arbitrage transactions, or by institutional investors who recognize a temporary price variation. If such price discrepancies persist for extended periods, the variations may no longer be considered temporary, and a contract can lose its hedging characteristics for selected debt instruments or securities.

Generally, a hedger or speculator will stand for delivery or make delivery only if he or she can redeliver or purchase the same commodity at a profit in the cash market. Opportunities for arbitrage occur frequently in GNMA securities since currently three contracts are traded, each with different delivery regulations.

It is now possible to selectively take delivery on the CBOT and redeliver these securities into the cash market or ACE in the same contract month. A seller no longer must be a regular originator in order to deliver GNMA securities collateralized by mortgage originations into the ACE or certificate delivery contracts. Therefore, a mortgage originator must be aware of all available prices if a mortgage banker is to be assured of optimum profits.

An opportunity may occur selectively to deliver certain GNMA coupons into the futures market at better prices than are available in the cash market. This is a function of futures pricing that is related to a mathematical algorithm. In the cash market, the prices of various GNMA coupons are sometimes a function of supply and demand. Temporarily, one coupon can be priced richer or cheaper than others. Par stops often are not enforced.

An investor will have occasion to identify moments when futures contracts provide the cheapest source of bonds or T-bills. At such times purchases can be made with deferred payments for extended periods of time at little cost. Only margins must be posted; capital must be available only at the time of delivery. This procedure is frequently cheaper than purchasing a security on margin.

A speculator seldom wishes to make or take delivery of any security since the motivation to trade is solely for speculative profit. In addition, the speculator frequently has insufficient funds or credit lines to take possession of the security.

For these reasons, in addition to the administrative procedures associated with deliveries on a commodity exchange, fewer than 2 percent of all contracts traded are normally settled by delivery. Because occasional deliveries take place, it is important that all participants understand how they can be made. The steps associated with deliveries are prescribed by the regulations of the respective commodity exchanges. The following information can serve only as a guide, since the rules and regulations pertaining to any contract change periodically.

MAKING AND TAKING DELIVERY ON INTEREST RATE FUTURES CONTRACTS[1]

Delivery of long-term U.S. Treasury bonds

Contract-grade bonds

The Chicago Board of Trade futures contract in long-term U.S. Treasury bonds specifies that the contract grade consists of:

1. Callable U.S. Treasury bonds that are not callable for at least 15 years.
2. Noncallable U.S. Treasury bonds that have a maturity of at least 15 years.

All bonds delivered against a single contract must be of the same issue.

To determine the last deliverable day for a given issue:

1. Determine the computation date for the bond. The computation date is the date upon which the bond is callable, if the bond is callable, or, in the event the bond is not callable, the computation date is the date the bond is payable.
2. Determine the last deliverable date by taking the computation date and subtracting 15 years.

By the above process, the last deliverable date may be determined for each issue. No issue may be delivered in satisfaction of a short position on a CBOT long-term U.S. Treasury bond contract after the last deliverable date for that issue.

---

[1] These rules are extracted from exchange regulations pertaining to delivery instructions of the respective contracts in effect on December 1978. They are subject to change.

Rules of the ACE GNMA Futures Contract, Amex Commodities Exchange, Inc., 1978.

Making and Taking Delivery on Interest Rate Futures Contracts, Chicago Board of Trade, 2d Revised Edition, 1977.

Futures Trading in U.S. Treasury Bills, Chicago Mercantile Exchange, November, 1977.

For example, on June 1, 1978 the following issues would be deliverable up to and including the dates given.

Issue	Call date	Payable	Last day deliverable
8½ 1994-99	May 15, 1994	May 15, 1999	May 15, 1979
3 1995	None	Feb. 15, 1995	Feb. 15, 1980
7⅞ 1995-00	Feb. 15, 1995	Feb. 15, 2000	Feb. 15, 1980
8⅜ 1995-00	Aug. 15, 1995	Aug. 15, 2000	Aug. 15, 1980
8 1996-01	Aug. 15, 1996	Aug. 15, 2001	Aug. 15, 1981
3½ 1998	None	Nov. 15, 1998	Nov. 15, 1983
8¼ 2000-05	May 15, 2000	May 15, 2005	May 15, 1985
7⅝ 2002-07	Feb. 15, 2002	Feb. 15, 2007	Feb. 15, 1987

Invoicing of long-term U.S. Treasury bond deliveries

The contract provides that on intention day (Day 2, as will be explained below), the short (seller) must invoice the long (buyer) for the contract of the bonds plus accrued interest. The invoice is to be on a form specified by the CBOT.

Principal. The contract provides for delivery of $100,000 principal of any issue of contract-grade bonds. The price at which the delivered issue will yield 8 percent at its current time to maturity (or, if callable, at its current time to call) is found in the bond table published by the Financial Publishing Company of Boston. In conjunction with the introduction of the long-term U.S. Treasury bond futures contract, the Financial Publishing Company published Treasury Bond Futures Conversion Factors, Publication No. 765. It contains factors for virtually every coupon rate and maturity or call date that is or may be available. Please note that if the price is not expressed as a decimal equivalent, it must be converted to one (see examples below).

This price is multiplied by the settlement price on position day (Day 1, as will be explained below), and by $100,000 (the contract size) in order to arrive at the principal invoice amount (see the example below).

The time to maturity or call for purposes of determining the multiplier found in the bond tables is calculated in complete three-month quarters, with no rounding up to the higher quarter, and is based on the first day of the delivery month. For example, an issue with 21 years, 4 months, and 17 days to call on the first day of the delivery month is assumed to have a time to call of 21 years and one quarter for purposes of invoice calculations.

As an example, assume that the 7⅝ percent bonds of February 15, 2007, are to be delivered on June 17, 1977, and the settlement price on position day was 99-15. On June 1, 1977, the 7⅝ percent bonds of February 2007 were callable in 24 years, 8 months, and 14 days, which translates into 24 years and two complete quarters, rounding down to the nearest quarter. In the 7⅝ percent coupon table of the Financial Publishing Company's bond book, the price to yield 8 percent in 24 years and two quarters is 96-00. The invoice amount for the principal would be:

0.9600000	Price of 7⅝ percent bonds to yield 8 percent in 24 years and two quarters
X 0.9946875	Decimal equivalent of position day
0.9549000	settlement price
X $100,000	Contract size
$95,490.00	Invoice principal amount

The price to yield 8 percent will change in the following delivery months because the time to call of the delivered issue will decrease. Thus, a delivery six months later at the same settlement price would result in a different invoice principal amount:

0.9603000	Price of 7⅝ percent bonds to yield 8 percent in 24 years
X 0.9946875	Decimal equivalent of position day
0.9551984	settlement price
X $100,000	Contract size
$95,519.84	Invoice principal amount

The invoice principal amount has increased by $29.84 because the price taken from the Financial Publishing Company's tables for a 24-year-to-call bond is different from that for a bond with 24 years and two quarters to call. Thus, someone who takes delivery of this issue in June and redelivers it in December at the same settlement price will receive $29.84 more for invoiced principal in December than he or she paid in June. It should be noted that changes in the invoiced principal are dependent on (1) the coupon to be delivered and (2) the time between delivery and redelivery. These factors can affect both the direction and the magnitude of change.

Accrued interest. The delivering short (seller) also must invoice the receiving long (buyer) for interest that has accrued but has not been paid as of the time of delivery. Accrued interest is to be determined in accordance with Department of Treasury Circular 300, Subpart P. Persons desiring details should consult that circular; the following is only a brief example of how the calculation would be done in one circumstance and is provided for general information only.

For example, the 7⅝'s of 2007 pay interest of February 15 and August 15. For delivery on June 17, there are 122 days counting from, but not including, February 15, to and including June 17. According to the half-year table in Treasury Circular 300, Subpart P, a regular year (i.e., not a leap year) contains 181 days from February to August. The accrued interest is calculated as follows:

$3,812.50	Semiannual interest payment ($100,000 × 7⅝% ÷ 2)
X 0.6740331	122/181 days
$2,569.75	Invoiced amount for accrued interest on June 17 delivery

Combining the figures from the examples the total amount for the June 17 delivery would be:

$95,490.00	Invoiced amount for principal
2,569.75	Invoiced amount for accrued interest
$98,059.75	Total invoice amount

Delivery of long-term U.S. Treasury bonds by book entry

In keeping with most cash market transactions in Treasury bonds, the long-term U.S. Treasury bond futures contract calls for delivery by book entry in accordance with Department of Treasury Circular 300, Subpart O: "Book-Entry Procedure." Persons desiring details of this system should consult that circular; the following is only a brief summary of it for general information.

The essence of the process is that the short (seller) and the long (buyer) perform their respective functions in the delivery process through agents that must be commercial banks, that are members of the Federal Reserve System, and that have capital (capital, surplus, and undivided earnings) in excess of $150 million.

The short may acquire book-entry Treasury bonds in three ways:

1. Purchase them for his or her own account through a Federal Reserve member bank.
2. Convert definitive (i.e., printed from U.S. Treasury) bonds to book-entry bonds by depositing them with a Federal Reserve member bank in accordance with Department of Treasury Circular 300, Subpart O. Converting definitive bonds to book-entry bonds usually can be accomplished in about a day, unless the bonds are registered, in which case it can take about five days.
3. Instruct an agent to purchase book-entry Treasury bonds.

Delivery on long-term U.S. Treasury bond futures is a three-day process. Delivery day (Day 3, see below) can be any business day in the month for which the contract calls for delivery. It should be noted that it is the short who elects the date of delivery by filing a Notice of Intention to Deliver.

Day 1 (position day). The short (seller) must give notice to a clearing member. The seller must notify the clearing member of the specific issue he or she intends to deliver. The bonds at this point must be in book-entry form. Before 8:00 P.M. on position day, the clearing member must file with the Board of Trade Clearing Corporation a Notice of Intention to Deliver, using the form specified by the CBOT.

Day 2 (intention day). The Clearing Corporation assigns the notice to the oldest outstanding long (buyer) of record. The long is notified by a clearing member:

1. That he has stopped the short's notice in U.S. Treasury bond futures (i.e., that the notice has been assigned to him as the oldest outstanding long of record).
2. The specific issue(s) he will receive.

3. The dollar amount invoiced, based upon the settlement price of Day 1, adjusted as explained above.

Day 3 (delivery day). In the event the long does not agree with the invoice amount, the long must notify his broker, who in turn will notify his clearing member, who must resolve the dispute with the short's clearing member by 9:30 A.M. By 12 noon, the short's clearing member notifies his bank to transfer Treasury bonds by book entry to the account of the long's clearing member and the dollar amount of the remittance. By 12 noon the long's clearing member notifies his bank to accept transfer of Treasury bonds by book entry and to remit in federal funds to the account of the short's clearing member at the short's bank.

Adjustment of traders' trading accounts

As shown above, invoicing for delivery purposes is based upon the settlement price on position day (Day 1). It is unlikely that this settlement price will be the same as that at which the delivering short originally sold or the receiving long originally bought. The differences that exist are handled by adjustment of the traders' respective trading accounts by the firm that carries the account. This adjustment is based on the settlement price of the position day.

For example, assume that the short who delivered had originally sold the futures contract at 95-00 and that the long who took delivery had originally bought that futures contract at 96-00. Though firms' bookkeeping methods vary, the adjustment for the short, in substance, would be:

Sold futures contract for	$95,000.00
Delivery based on settlement price of	99,468.75
Debit against trader's account	$ 4,468.75

The prices have been converted to dollar amounts based on $100,000 principal for ease of analysis. For the long, the calculations would be:

Bought futures contract for	$96,000.00
Delivery based on settlement price of	99,468.75
Credit to trader's account	$ 3,468.75

The above examples do not include commissions or exchange service fees. It is the settlement price, not the invoice amount, that is used for adjustment of the account.

As one can see, through this method the short's and long's respective net financial positions are adjusted to approximately those at which they originally contracted. (There will be some discrepancy, because the account also reflects the transfer of funds made on delivery, which included the apportioning of accrued interest, the adjustment for the coupon, and the adjustment for the coupon rate of bonds delivered. The original contract price did not include these factors. However, as is obvious, these adjustments are valid in light of what each party in fact gave and/or received. Also, each account is debited for commissions and exchange service fees.)

Through this method, the short and the long are not confined to delivery with the same parties with whom they made their original trade, nor even to parties whose trades were made at the same price. The use of the settlement price in delivery invoicing and in adjusting traders' accounts interfaces with the usual margining and accounting systems for traders who offset their trades prior to delivery. Those traders (such as, perhaps, the long who bought from our short originally and the short who sold to our long originally) have been free to close out their positions with subsequent offsetting trades at such prices as they could obtain. When they did, their accounts, too, would have been adjusted accordingly, using the price of each offsetting trade in place of the settlement price in the deliverer's and receiver's adjustments above. Because there is a buyer for each seller and a receiver for each deliverer, through this system each person's account reflects his or her own transactions, and the net result is that all transactions cancel out. In the meantime, a liquid market is maintained and facilitated.

Origination and delivery of collateralized depository receipts under the GNMA mortgage interest rate futures contract

Origination of CDRs

The GNMA mortgage interest rate futures contract does not allow for direct delivery of GNMA certificates in settlement of a futures position. Instead, the contract calls for delivery of an instrument called a collateralized depository receipt (CDR). A CDR is a document prepared, signed, and dated by the depository to reflect the fact that the originator has placed in safekeeping $100,000 minimum principal balance of GNMA 8's or equivalent on the date so indicated (see Exhibit C).

Any individual can deliver or receive CDRs in the futures market via a broker or a clearing member, but only regular originators can originate or create CDRs. The origination process of CDRs is described in this section. The process of delivery is described later in this chapter.

CDRs can be originated only by organizations classified as regular for origination by the CBOT. An organization wishing to become regular for origination must deposit $1,000 face value of Treasury bills with the CBOT. This application cycle takes 30-60 days. Regularity for origination takes effect 30 days after all terms and conditions have been met and notice to that effect has been posted on the bulletin board of the CBOT.

To originate CDRs, a regular originator deposits a certain principal balance of GNMA securities in a depository approved by the CBOT. Depositories must be U.S. banks with capital in excess of $100 million, must maintain offices or correspondent banks in the immediate vicinity of the CBOT, and must be approved by the CBOT to act as depositories.

The amount of GNMA securities placed in safekeeping must be at least $100,000 principal balance of GNMA 8's, or an amount of other interest rate GNMAs to give a yield equivalent to that of a principal balance of $100,000 of GNMA 8's when calculated at par under the assumptions of a 30-year certificate prepaid in the twelfth year. The following tabulation gives the equivalants for the most popular GNMA coupons. The originator could choose, for example, to deposit $93,168 of GNMA 9's or $112,124 of GNMA 6.5's into an approved deposit account. The originator can deposit more than one GNMA to make up the $100,000 or equivalent. If the originator chose to originate ten CDRs, he or she could deposit one GNMA 8 with a principal balance of $1 million minimum, or any number of GNMA securities that have a combined equivalent principal balance of $1 million minimum.

When the GNMA securities have been re-registered in the name of the depository or its nominee, the depository will give the originator a CDR, which the depository will sign to warrant that at the time the CDR was signed there was, in safekeeping, $100,000 principal balance minimum of GNMA 8's or equivalent.

The originator will present this CDR to the Registrar of the CBOT and, when signed by the Registrar, the CDR becomes an instrument deliverable against futures contracts.

Calculation of equivalent principal balances

An amount of GNMA securities bearing a stated interest rate other than 8 percent can be converted to an "equivalent principal balance" of GNMA 8's using the following formula:

$$\frac{\text{Principal balance of GNMA } X\text{'s}}{\text{Conversion factor for GNMA } X\text{'s}} = \begin{array}{c}\text{Equivalent} \\ \text{principal balance} \\ \text{of GNMA 8's}\end{array}$$

A conversion factor is the amount of a particular GNMA security required to give a yield equal to the yield on $1.00 of GNMA 8's when priced at par and under the assumptions of a 30-year certificate prepaid in the twelfth year. Table 4-7 depicts the appropriate conversion factors for GNMA securities with the most common interest rates.

Examples

A $37,394 principal balance of GNMA 6.5's is equivalent to:

$$\frac{37,394}{1.121233} = \$33,350.78 \text{ of GNMA 8's}$$

A $308,291 principal balance of GNMA 8.5's is equivalent to:

$$\frac{308,291}{0.965018} = \$319,466.57 \text{ of GNMA 8's}$$

Registration and delivery of CDRs

An originator can register CDRs with the Registrar of the CBOT during any business day. A CDR must be endorsed by an approved depository before the CDR will be registered by the Registrar. Once a CDR has been registered by the Registrar, it is eligible for delivery in satisfaction of a short position in the futures market.

A CDR can be transferred from one party to another outside of the futures market. It also can be delivered and redelivered into the futures market in satisfaction of subsequent owners' short positions. However, before each delivery can take place, the CDR must be endorsed by the clearing member making delivery to confirm proper title to the CDR. In addition, prior to each delivery, the CDR must be endorsed by the depository to warrant that it is a genuine CDR. The clearing member making delivery is responsible for obtaining the depository's endorsement. When both of these endorsements have been added to the CDR, it can be delivered in the futures market.

Delivery can be made on any business day of the month in which the futures contract calls for delivery. However, intention day is one business day prior to delivery, and the Notice of Intention to Deliver must be filed by the short's clearing member with the Board of Trade Clearing Corporation by 8:00 P.M. on the business day preceding intention day.

The short (seller) elects to make delivery by filing a Notice of Intention to Deliver through a clearing member, using a form as specified by the CBOT. On the following morning (intention day), the Clearing Corporation assigns the notice to the oldest outstanding long (buyer) of record, and each party is informed of who the opposite clearing member is.

Later on intention day, using a form specified by the CBOT, the clearing member of the delivering short presents to the clearing member of the receiving long an invoice of the amount due and payable by the long on delivery day. This amount is based on the settlement price on position day (the day the short filed the

Notice of Intention to Deliver with the Clearing Corporation), plus accrued interest prorated from the first day of the delivery month to and including the date of delivery of the CDR. (In case of prepayments of interest, prorated adjustments must be made. Payment of interest on CDRs in general is discussed below.)

On delivery day, through their respective clearing members, the long pays the invoice amount by certified or cashier's check drawn on a Chicago bank in same-day funds in U.S. currency, and the short delivers the CDR.

Adjustment of traders' trading accounts

As indicated above, payment for delivery purposes is based on the settlement price on position day, the day on which the Notice of Intention to Deliver is given by the delivering short. It is unlikely that this settlement price will be the same as the price at which either the delivering short or the receiving long originally made the futures contract trades. The differences that exist are handled by adjustment of the traders' respective trading accounts by the firm that carries the account. This adjustment is based on the settlement price of the position day.

Assume, for example, that delivery was made based on a settlement price of 96-00, that the long had originally bought at 97-00, and that the short had originally sold at 98-00. Though firms' bookkeeping methods vary, the adjustment of the long's trading account would, in substance, be:

Bought futures at	$97,000
Took delivery at	96,000
Debit against trading account	$ 1,000

The short's trading account would be adjusted:

Sold futures at	$98,000
Made delivery for	96,000
Credit to trading account	$ 2,000

The above examples do not include commissions or exchange

service fees. Prices have been converted to dollar amounts based on one contract for ease of analysis.

As one can see, through this method the short's and the long's respective net financial positions are adjusted to approximately those at which they originally contracted. (There is some discrepancy due to apportioning of accrued interest on the delivery invoice, and due to the member firm's deduction of commissions and exchange service fees.)

Through this method, the short and the long are not confined to delivery with the same parties with whom they made their original trades, nor even to parties whose trades were made at the same prices. The use of the settlement price in delivery invoicing and in adjusting traders' accounts meshes with the usual margining and accounting systems for traders who offset their trades prior to delivery. Those traders (such as, perhaps, the long who bought from our short originally and the short who sold to our long originally) have been free to close out their positions with subsequent offsetting trades at such prices as they could obtain. When they did, their accounts, too, would have been adjusted accordingly, using the price of each offsetting trade in place of the settlement price in the deliverer's and receiver's adjustments above. Because there is a buyer for each seller and a receiver for each deliverer, through this system each person's account reflects his or her own transactions, and the net result is that all transactions cancel out. In the meantime, a liquid market is maintained and facilitated.

Originator's duties after origination of CDRs

The originator must pay $635 interest on the second to last business day of each month to the holder of each CDR when the CDR is presented at the depository of a correspondent bank.

The principal balance of GNMA securities in the deposit account must be maintained at $100,000 minimum of GNMA 8's or equivalent per CDR. Therefore, if a principal payment reduces the principal balance below $100,000 GNMA 8's or equivalent, the originator must deposit additional GNMA securities in the deposit account.

For example, assume the originator originally placed $94,000 of GNMA 9's in safekeeping and a principal payment reduces the principal balance to $92,000. The originator now has in safekeeping:

$$\frac{\$92,000}{0.931677} = \$98,746.67 \text{ of GNMA 8's equivalent}$$

The originator must therefore deposit an additional $1,253.33 minimum principal balance of GNMA 8's or equivalent.

On the last interest payment date prior to the CDR becoming one year old, the holder will present the CDR to the originator for renewal. The originator is obliged to present the holder with another duly registered CDR with at least one remaining interest payment. The replacement CDR can be originated either by the original originator or by any other regular originator. In other words, if a particular originator wishes to fully retire her CDRs, she can do so by replacing her old CDRs with new CDRs purchased from other originators.

If by any means an originator ever regains control of an outstanding CDR originated by himself, he must immediately cancel the registration of that CDR.

At any time during their life, CDRs can be surrendered to the originator for GNMA certificates. The procedure is discussed below.

Surrender of CDRs

During any business day, the holder of a CDR can surrender the CDR for GNMA certificates at the office of the depository or correspondent bank. The depository must inform the CDR originator that a CDR has been surrendered. The originator then must inform the depository how he wishes to satisfy the obligations under the CDR. The GNMA securities to be delivered do not necessarily have to be provided from those in safekeeping and can be from any pool bearing any stated interest rate the originator may choose.

Whatever source the originator chooses, there must be sufficient GNMA securities to satisfy the obligations within 15 business days after surrender of the CDR. The originator must provide between $97,500 and $102,500 principal balance of GNMA 8's or equivalent per CDR (i.e., within a ±2.5 percent tolerance limit of $100,000. Discrepancies within the tolerance limit are settled between the originator and the bearer through a cash transaction at par. Principal balance equivalents for certificates with stated interest rates other than 8 percent are calculated as explained above.

For example, assume a CDR is surrendered and the originator decides to provide $94,700 principal balance of GNMA 9's, which are purchased from a GNMA dealer. This is equivalent to:

$$\frac{\$94,700}{0.931677} = \$101,644.67 \text{ of GNMA 8's}$$

The party who surrendered the CDR therefore gives the originator $1,644.67 ($101,644.67 − $100,000) in cash to settle the balance.

Alternatively, the originator could have provided $109,900 of GNMA 6.5's. This would have been equivalent to:

$$\frac{\$109,900}{1.121233} = \$98,017.09 \text{ of GNMA 8's}$$

The originator would therefore provide an additional $1,982.91 ($100,000 − $98,017.09) in cash to the party who surrendered the CDR.

The originator can provide any number of GNMA certificates upon surrender of a single CDR. There can also be a single certificate for several CDRs, provided that the CDRs are surrendered by a single holder and the principal balance equivalent of the GNMA being provided is within ±2.5 percent of the total in the CDRs (balance settled in cash as above).

Figure 7-1 is a schematic diagram of the origination, delivery, and surrender of CDRs.

108

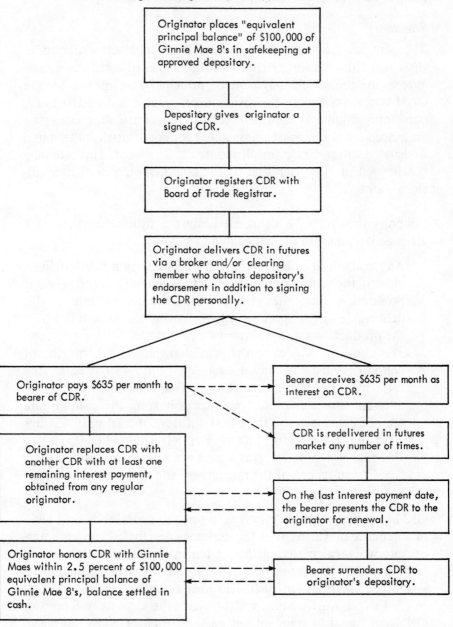

Figure 7-1
Schematic diagram of origination, delivery, and surrender of CDRs

Originator places "equivalent principal balance" of $100,000 of Ginnie Mae 8's in safekeeping at approved depository.

Depository gives originator a signed CDR.

Originator registers CDR with Board of Trade Registrar.

Originator delivers CDR in futures via a broker and/or clearing member who obtains depository's endorsement in addition to signing the CDR personally.

Originator pays $635 per month to bearer of CDR.

Bearer receives $635 per month as interest on CDR.

CDR is redelivered in futures market any number of times.

Originator replaces CDR with another CDR with at least one remaining interest payment, obtained from any regular originator.

On the last interest payment date, the bearer presents the CDR to the originator for renewal.

Originator honors CDR with Ginnie Maes within 2.5 percent of $100,000 equivalent principal balance of Ginnie Mae 8's, balance settled in cash.

Bearer surrenders CDR to originator's depository.

Source: *CBOT Delivery Manual,* © 1977, Chicago Board of Trade.

109

Organization and delivery of certificate delivery GNMA interest rate futures on the Chicago Board of Trade

Standards

The contract grade for delivery on futures contracts made under these regulations is single-family mortgage-backed certificates guaranteed for the timely payment of principal and interest by the GNMA as described in the standard prospectus form HUD-1717, commonly known as modified pass-through certificates. Deliveries are priced on the basis of a designated coupon. Initially, the stated designated interest rate for all months is 8 percent. This rate may be changed at the discretion of the board, should market conditions warrant.

Coupons that may be delivered against a futures contract in a given delivery month are designated as follows:

1. Any coupon at or below the current production rate is deliverable. If the current production rate is lower than the previous production rate, then the previous production rate is also deliverable in the three months following the month in which the production rate was lowered.
2. The above is subject to the provision that no substitution of coupon is made for any delivery date until 45 days after the effective date of the rate change. That is, if the current production rate is changed, certificates bearing the coupon rate are not deliverable on the CBOT futures contract until 45 days after the new coupon rate is in effect. The one exception to this rule is the delivery of a new issue dated and issued after the date of record of the rate change and bearing the new rate.

GNMAs delivered are adjusted as to price to provide for firm yield maintenance on the basis of the exchange-designated coupon interest rate when calculated at the settlement price on the last day of trading under the assumption of a 30-year mortgage prepaid in 12 years. [Calculations on such deliveries are made as follows: The price at which the delivered GNMA yields the same as an 8 percent GNMA is found in standard net yield tables for GNMA mortgage-backed securities as published by the Financial Publishing Company of Boston. If the yield and price fall between two quoted prices (i.e., an increment less than 1/32), the price should be interpolated linearly.]

Liquidation during the delivery month

After trading in contracts for future delivery in the current delivery month has ceased, outstanding contracts for such delivery may be liquidated by the delivery, on delivery day, of GNMA certificates meeting the standards prescribed, or by mutual agreement by means of a bona fide exchange of such current futures for GNMA certificates or a comparable instrument. Such exchange must, in any event, be made no later than noon (1:00 P.M. EST) on the fourth business day prior to the delivery day. Further, the long clearing member must transmit to the Clearing Corporation on the fourth business day prior to the delivery day by 8:00 P.M. (9:00 P.M. EST), in addition to other data normally submitted, the position of every long customer and the house long position.

Notice of Intention to Deliver

The position day (the day on which notice is given) is three business days before the delivery day. Any short who has an open position on position day is required to deposit the requisite amount of GNMA certificates with the agent by 2:00 P.M. (3:00 P.M. EST) on position day. The CBOT transmits open interest information to the agent by 10:00 A.M. (11:00 A.M. EST) on position day. Such information includes the names of all short and long clearing members, and the open positions of each short and long.

Invoicing

The agent matches the long and short positions by noon on service day, the business day before the delivery day, and sends to each long and short the respective matching. The short clearing member then invoices the long clearing member (and sends a copy to the agent) before 3:00 P.M. (4:00 P.M. EST) on the service day. The invoice includes the following information: the coupon(s) of the GNMAs being delivered, the pool number(s), the factor, the prorated interest payment charged by the short to the long, and the invoice amount. In the event the long does not agree with the terms of the invoice received from the short, the long must notify the short, and the dispute must be settled before the start of business on the delivery day.

Deliveries of futures contracts

Deliveries against GNMA futures contracts must be by actual GNMA certificates meeting the standards prescribed. Interest accrued on the GNMAs delivered is charged to the long clearing member by the short clearing member, prorated from the first day of the delivery month to the date of delivery of the GNMAs.

The delivery day is the 16th of the delivery month, unless the 16th is a holiday or weekend day, in which case the delivery day is the first business day prior to the 16th. All deliveries must be made through and assigned by the Clearing Corporation. Where a commission house as a member of the Clearing Corporation has both long and short interests for customers on its own books, it must tender to the Clearing Corporation such Notices of Intention to Deliver as it received from its customers who are short.

By noon (1:00 P.M. EST) on delivery day, the agent must deposit the funds into an account designated by the short clearing member and transfer the GNMAs to the long clearing member or a designate.

Deliveries may include no more than one pool of a current deliverable grade of GNMA certificates per contract delivered. They should include certificates in such face amounts and remaining principal balances that the agent can break the certificates into contract-size pieces (i.e. face amounts that can be broken into individual contract-size pieces that meet GNMA requirements for minimum increments of face amount and minimum size for tail pieces[2] as well as the remaining principal balance requirements on a per-contract basis). A maximum delivery variance of ±2.5 percent of the remaining principal balance of the aggregate face value for each contract deliverable is permitted on a per-contract basis.

---

[2] Tail piece is the remaining amount of face value of a pool in excess of $1,000,000.

112

Payment

Payment must be made in federal funds. The long must deposit the funds with the agent by 10:00 A.M. (11:00 A.M. EST) on the delivery day.

Organization and delivery of certificate delivery GNMA interest rate futures on the American Commodities Exchange

Standards

The contract grade for delivery on futures contracts made under these regulations is single-family mortgage-backed certificates guaranteed for the timely payment of principal and interest by the GNMA as described in the standard prospectus form HUD-1717, commonly known as modified pass-through certificates, and bearing the stated coupon interest rate designated by the exchange as the current deliverable grade for that delivery month at the time that delivery month is initiated for trading. The initial designated interest rate for all months is 8 percent.

Certificates bearing coupon interest rates other than the stated rate designated by the exchange are deliverable in satisfaction of these contracts provided that:

1. GNMAs delivered be adjusted as to price to provide for firm yield maintenance on the basis of the exchange-designated coupon interest rate when calculated at par under the assumption of a 30-year mortgage with a 12-year average life. [Calculations on such deliveries are made as follows: The price at which the delivered GNMA, if other than the designated rate, will yield the same as the designated rate can be found in standard net yield tables for GNMA mortgage-backed securities as published by the Financial Publishing Company of Boston. If the yield and price fall between two quoted prices (i.e., an increment less than 1/32), the price should be interpolated linearly.]
2. GNMAs bearing a coupon rate higher than the exchange-designated interest rate are not deliverable if the adjusted firm yield maintenance price is more than 100 percent of par,

113

except where such coupon rate represents the current production rate of new GNMA certificates as called for by the FHA/VA mortgage ceiling rate.

3. GNMAs bearing a coupon rate lower than the exchange-designated coupon interest rate are deliverable in accordance with the rules presented here.

The seller must deliver in accordance with the following specifications based on the number of contracts to be delivered for each single account on the books of the clearing member:

1. Single accounts delivering amounts equal to ten or more contracts must make separate deliveries for each unit of ten contracts and for the amount by which the number of contracts exceeds multiples of ten contracts in accordance with the provisions of this contract governing such deliveries.

2. Delivery for each multiple of ten contracts must be made in certificates representing not more than two pools, with an aggregate total remaining principal balance of $1 million and a maximum total variance of ±2.5 percent.

3. Single accounts delivering positions of less than ten contracts or the number of contracts in excess of multiples of ten contracts must deliver certificates representing not more than one pool, with an aggregate remaining principal balance of the number of contracts delivered multiplied by $100,000, with a maximum total variance of ±2.5 percent for each position delivered.

Last day of trading

No trades in GNMA futures deliverable in the current month may be made after the third Tuesday of that month, or the first exchange business day thereafter if the third Tuesday is a nonbusiness day. When necessary to facilitate the re-registration of securities at the end of the month, the board may establish an alternate date for the last day of trading.

Deliveries on futures contracts

No deliveries may be made in a current delivery month except on the day specified for such delivery in this contract. At the conclusion of trading in the delivery month, all open positions must be satisfied by the actual delivery of GNMA certificates that meet the standards and regulations of the Clearing Corporation.

Tender of delivery notice

A clearing member holding open positions in the contract in the current month at the time trading in that contract has ceased must deliver to the Clearing Corporation on a prescribed form details of the number of individual accounts, including those in omnibus accounts, and the number of contracts long or short in each not later than 10:00 A.M. of the exchange business day following the last day of trading in that contract.

The Clearing Corporation matches individual buyer and seller positions in accordance with the following priorities.

1. Buyers and sellers of positions of ten contracts or multiples thereof are matched first. If the remaining unmatched positions of ten contracts or multiples thereof are buyers, the Clearing Corporation matches sellers to buyers in such manner as to provide buyers with a minimum number of separate pool certificates in effecting the delivery.
2. Buyers and sellers of individual positions of fewer than ten contracts are matched after positions of ten have been matched in order of the size of the positions. The match is effected so as to provide such buyers with the minimum number of separate pool certificates for each position held.

   In the event that the Clearing Corporation is unable to effect an even match of buyer and seller positions, it may require such sellers as it selects to deliver certificates in such amounts as will enable the Clearing Corporation to effect a match in accordance with these rules. Sellers who are required to split delivery positions must deliver certificates in required denominations that meet all the requirements of good delivery under these rules for the number of contracts in each separate portion of the split delivery. If the Clearing Corporation requires that a seller split a delivery position, the Clearing Corporation, upon presentation of necessary documentation and receipts, credits the seller with the direct cost assessed by the transfer agent for effecting such split. In selecting sellers who are required to split delivery positions, the Clearing Corporation uses a random number assignment procedure in order to provide a fair allocation of such requirements.

4. The Clearing Corporation advises clearing members not later than 9:00 A.M. on the second exchange business day following the last day of trading in the contract of any delivery positions that the Clearing Corporation may require splitting in order to match buyers with sellers.

Clearing members who hold open short positions must furnish delivery notices to the Clearing Corporation not later than 9:00 A.M. on the exchange business day prior to the day of delivery. Such delivery notices provide the details of the certificates that clearing members will deliver in satisfying these rules, in accordance with the procedures and on such forms as are required by the Clearing Corporation.

The Clearing Corporation will advise clearing members who hold open long positions of the details and settlement amounts of each delivery, based on the settlement price established on the last day of trading in the delivery month, no later than 2:00 P.M. on the exchange business day prior to the delivery date.

Delivery through the American Commodity Clearing Corporation

Delivery of GNMA certificates as required by these rules must be made on the fifth exchange business day following the last day of trading. All deliveries must be made through and assigned by the Clearing Corporation.

Interest accrued on the GNMAs delivered is charged to the buying clearing member by the selling clearing member and is prorated from the first day of the delivery month to the date of delivery of the GNMAs. In case of prepayment of interest, prorated adjustments are made.

Sellers who have given the Clearing Corporation a delivery notice in accordance with these rules and those of the Clearing Corporation must deliver to the Clearing Corporation the GNMA certificates that are specified in the delivery notice, properly endorsed, and in good transferable form in accordance with the regulations of the Department of Housing and Urban Development, GNMA,

116

and the U.S. Treasury Department general regulations with respect to U.S. government securities as contained in applicable department circulars.[3] This will be done no later than 11:00 A.M. on the fifth exchange business day after the last day of trading. The delivering clearing member must provide the Clearing Corporation with an account number at the clearing member's bank so that the Clearing Corporation can remit in federal funds the settlement amount for the delivery. Payments are credited to the clearing member accounts no later than 12:30 P.M. on the last day of delivery.

Payment by buyer

A clearing member who is receiving delivery must arrange for a clearing bank to remit in federal funds to the account of the Clearing Corporation's designated bank, the settlement amount as computed by the Clearing Corporation. Such payments must be credited to the Clearing Corporation's account not later than 11:00 A.M. on the day of delivery. Clearing members in receipt of delivery notices receive those GNMA certificates specified in the delivery notice from the Clearing Corporation by 12:30 P.M. of the delivery date.

Exchange for physicals

An exchange of actual GNMA certificates for GNMA futures contracts is permitted between or among members. Only clearing members who have been matched by the Clearing Corporation may enter into an exchange for physicals after trading in the current delivery month has ceased. Such exchange must be completed and the Clearing Corporation advised not later than 9:00 A.M. on the exchange business day prior to the delivery day.

Delivery of 90-day T-bill under the T-bill futures contract

Contract-grade T-bills

Each contract must be for a T-bill with a remaining maturity of 90 days and a face value of $1 million. At the seller's option, a delivery unit may be composed of U.S. T-bills bearing maturities of 91 or 92 days. All bills in a delivery must have uniform maturity

---

[3] Currently U.S. Treasury Department Circular No. 300.

dates. The following formula may be used to calculate the value of a delivery unit:

$$\text{Dollar value} = \$1,000,000 - \left(\frac{\text{Days to maturity}}{360} \times \text{T-bill yield} \times \$1,000,000\right)$$

Delivery dates

Delivery must be made on the business day following the last day of trading, unless that day is an IMM or Illinois bank holiday. In that case, delivery is on the next business day common to the IMM and Illinois banks.

Termination of trading of contracts occurs on the second business day following the Federal Reserve 3-month (13-week) Treasury bill auction in the third week of the delivery month. In the event that no auction takes place, trading terminates on the third Wednesday of the contract month. For the purpose of this rule, the third week of the delivery month is the week commencing on the third Monday of the delivery month.

Invoicing

Payment. The clearinghouse monitors the delivery procedures to insure the proper transfer of Treasury bills and direct payment by the buyer to the seller. Payment must be made on the basis of par value, $1 million, minus yield, expressed in dollars, as determined by the settling price of the futures contract, discounted from the final settlement date to the maturity date on the basis of a 360-day year.

Costs of delivery are the responsibility of the seller.

Transaction procedures

Seller's duties. The clearing member representing the seller must deliver to the IMM clearinghouse by 12 noon (Chicago time) on the last day of trading a seller's delivery commitment indicating a Chicago bank that is registered with the IMM and a member of the Federal Reserve System, and the name of the account from which the delivery will be transferred. By 11:00 A.M. (Chicago time) on the day of delivery, the seller must deliver to a Chicago bank that is registered with the IMM, a member of the Federal Reserve System, and selected by the buyer, a U.S. Treasury bill maturing in 90 days with a face value at maturity of $1 million.

Buyer's duties. The clearing member representing the buyer must deliver to the clearinghouse by 12 noon (Chicago time) on the last day of trading a buyer's delivery commitment including the buyer's name and account number, and the name of a Chicago bank that is registered with the IMM and a member of the Federal Reserve System, to which delivery of the T-bill should be made. By 11:00 A.M. (Chicago time) on the day of delivery, the selling clearing member's bank or its designated agent must receive a wire transfer of federal funds for the net invoice amount.

Delivery of financial receipts under the 90-day commercial paper loan futures contract

Important general features of the contract

The unique feature of the CBOT commercial paper loan futures contract is that the long contracts to deliver commercial paper to the short and the short contracts to pay cash to the long. This is contrary to all other commodity futures contracts, in which the short makes delivery of the commodity. If this causes philosophical problems, perhaps a better way of looking at this contract is that it is a contract for a loan, and the short makes delivery of the loan while the long pays in commercial paper.

Also unique to this contract is that the long initiates the delivery process by giving a Notice of Intention to Deliver to the Board of Trade Clearing Corporation. In other contracts, the short initiates the delivery process by giving notice.

The commercial paper loan futures contract does not allow for direct delivery of commercial paper in settlement of a long futures position. Instead, the contract calls for delivery of a financial receipt created by a clearing member (a member of the Clearing Corporation) who has placed sufficient contract-grade commercial paper in an approved vault. (This is somewhat analogous to other futures contracts, except long-term U.S. Treasury bond futures, which allow direct delivery by book entry.) It should be pointed out that, through a clearing member, any person can make delivery of financial receipts in satisfaction of a long position, but only clearing members can create financial receipts.

Contract-grade commercial paper

Under the CBOT 90-day commercial paper loan futures contract, contract-grade commercial paper is limited to paper that (1) is rated A-1 by Standard & Poor's Corporation, (2) is rated P-1 by Moody's Investors Service, Inc., and (3) has been approved as deliverable by the CBOT. All three of these requirements must be met both at the time the financial receipt is created and at the time it is delivered.

In addition, deliverable commercial paper is limited to paper maturing on a business day not more than 90 days from the date on which delivery of the financial receipt is made. It should be noted that (1) the paper need not be new 90-day commercial paper (for example, originally it could have been 180-day paper that now has 90 days to go), (2) the paper can mature in less than 90 days (but the invoice amount is still calculated on the basis of a 90-day maturity), and (3) the 90-day figure is based on the date on which the financial receipt is delivered (not the date on which it is created, or the date on which it is surrendered for the commercial paper).

Parties who are unsure whether a specific corporation's issue of commercial paper meets the requirements described above should contact their clearing member or the Office of the Secretary of the Chicago Board of Trade.

Creation of financial receipts

A financial receipt is a document prepared, signed, and dated by an approved vault to show that a clearing member has placed $1 million of contract-grade commercial paper in safekeeping on the date indicated. It also indicates the issue placed in safekeeping.

The commercial paper placed in safekeeping at the vault may deviate from contract grade with respect to days to maturity at the time the financial receipt is created. The clearing member may create a financial receipt with contract-grade paper that has a

120

maturity beyond 90 days, but the financial receipt is not deliverable in the futures market until the underlying commercial paper has declined to a time to maturity of 90 days or less (counting both the day of delivery of the financial receipt and the day on which the commercial paper matures).

Financial receipts can be created only by clearing members of the CBOT.

Vaults in which commercial paper is placed for safekeeping and which issue financial receipts must be approved as regular vaults by the CBOT. Vaults must be U.S. banks with capital in excess of $150 million and must maintain offices or correspondent banks in the immediate vicinity of the CBOT.

When the commercial paper has been placed in safekeeping in an approved vault, the vault gives the clearing member a financial receipt signed to warrant that there is in safekeeping $1 million face value of commercial paper.

When a financial receipt is created, the clearing member creating the financial receipt pays all charges associated with creating it, storing commercial paper in the vault, and surrendering the financial receipt for commercial paper.

The clearing member will present the financial receipt to the Registrar of the CBOT and, when signed by the Registrar, the financial receipt becomes an instrument deliverable against long futures positions on or after the date indicated on the face of the instrument (the date the underlying paper becomes 90-day paper).

Each financial receipt is deliverable only when the commercial paper backing that receipt has 90 days or less to maturity. However, even though a financial receipt may not yet be deliverable in the futures market, it is still a valid receipt for the commercial paper held in safekeeping.

A financial receipt can be transferred from one party to another outside of the futures market. The clearing member through whom delivery is made need not be the same clearing member who created the financial receipt. A financial receipt can be delivered and redelivered in satisfaction of subsequent owners' long positions, but, again, there is no adjustment for the fact that the underlying commercial paper would have less than 90 days to maturity when the financial receipt is redelivered.

Registration and delivery of financial receipts

A financial receipt must be endorsed by an approved vault before it will be registered by the Registrar. To be eligible for delivery into the futures market, it must be registered by the Registrar. A clearing member can register financial receipts during any business day. Before delivering a properly registered financial receipt in satisfaction of a long position, the clearing member making delivery must endorse the financial receipt to confirm that he or she has proper title to it.

Delivery of financial receipts can be made on any business day during the month for which the contract calls for delivery. However, before 8:00 P.M. on the second business day prior to the delivery day, the long, through a clearing member, must file a Notice of Intention to Deliver with the Board of Trade Clearing Corporation, using a form as specified by the CBOT. This date on which the long files the notice is known as position day.

On the morning after the position day, the Clearing Corporation assigns the notice to the oldest outstanding short of record. Each party is informed of who the opposite clearing member is. This date is known as the intention day. Later that day, the clearing member of the long presents an invoice, using a form specified by the CBOT, to the clearing member of the short for the amount due and payable on delivery day.

By 12 noon on the following day (delivery day), the short pays to the long, through their respective clearing members (but not the Clearing Corporation), $1 million minus the quarterly equivalent of the settlement price on position day. Payment is by certified or cashier's check drawn on a Chicago bank of same-day funds in U.S. currency. The long delivers to the short a financial receipt.

For example, assume that on position day the settlement price was 5.29 percent. The short would pay the long:

$$\$1,000,000 - \left(\$1,000,000 \times \frac{90}{360} \times \frac{5.29}{100}\right) = \$986,775.00$$

Although a properly registered and endorsed financial receipt backed by contract-grade commercial paper with less than 90 days to maturity may be delivered into the futures market in satisfaction of a long position, settlement always is made on the basis of 90 days. Any loss of interest due to the fact that the paper is less than 90-day paper is borne solely by the long who elects to deliver a financial receipt backed by such paper.

For example, if a long delivers a financial receipt backed by commercial paper with 85 days to maturity and the settlement price is 6.00 percent, the long will receive from the short:

$$\$1,000,000 \times \left[1 - \left(\frac{90}{360} \times \frac{6.00}{100}\right)\right] = \$985,000$$

not

$$\$1,000,000 \times \left[1 - \left(\frac{85}{360} \times \frac{6.00}{100}\right)\right] = \$985,833$$

The five days of interest which the long loses by delivering a financial receipt backed by 85-day paper amounts to $833, or about $167 per day for this example, using a settlement price of 6.00 percent.

Adjustment of traders' trading accounts

As indicated above, settlement for delivery purposes is based upon the settlement price for the day on which the Notice of Intention to Deliver is given. It is unlikely that this settlement price will be the same as that at which either the delivering long or the receiving short originally made the respective contracts. The differences that exist are handled by adjustment of the traders' respective trading accounts by the firm that carries the account. This adjustment is based on the settlement price of the position day.

For example, assume that the long who delivered had originally contracted at 6.00 percent and that the short who received the financial receipt had originally contracted at 5.00 percent. Yet the delivery between them was settled based on the settlement price of 5.29 percent. Though firms' bookkeeping methods vary, the adjustment for the long's trading account would, in substance, be as follows:

Went long in futures at	6.00%
Made delivery at settlement price of	5.29
Debit to trading account	0.71%, or 71 basis points

Each basis point (0.01 percent) in commercial paper loan futures is worth $25.00 ($1 million contract size divided by 100 to get the value per 1 percent, then divided by 100 again to get the value per 0.01 percent, then divided by 4 because the paper is a 90-day, not yearly, instrument). Thus, the long's trading account would be credited with $1,775. For the short the calculations would be:

Went short in futures at	5.00%
Took delivery at settlement price of	5.29
Debit to trading account	0.29%, or 29 basis points

Thus, the short's trading account would be debited $725 (29 basis points times $25). The above examples do not include commissions, exchange service fees, or any fees the clearing member may charge for creating the financial receipt. Why did both sides receive a debit to the trading account? Because the settlement price happened to be both cheaper than that at which the long had originally contracted to deliver and more expensive than that at which the short had contracted to pay. If both of the original contracts had been at either less than 5.29 percent or more than 5.29 percent, one party would have had a credit and the other a debit.

As one can see, through this method the short's and the long's net financial positions are adjusted to be those at which they originally contracted (before deducting commissions and related fees pointed out above).

By this method, the short and long are not confined to delivery with the same parties with whom they made their original trades, nor even to parties whose trades were made at the same price. The use of the settlement price in settling deliveries interfaces with the usual margining and accounting systems for traders who offset their trades prior to delivery. Those traders (such as, perhaps, the long who contracted with our short above and the short who contracted with our long) have been free to close out their positions with subsequent offsetting trades at such prices as they could obtain. When they did, their accounts, too, would have been adjusted accordingly, using the price of the offsetting trade in place of the settlement price used in delivery adjustments. Because there is a buyer for each seller and a receiver for each deliverer, through this system each person's account reflects his or her own transactions and the net result is that all transactions cancel out. In the meantime, a liquid market is maintained and facilitated.

Surrender of financial receipts for commercial paper

A holder of a financial receipt who wishes to surrender it for commercial paper must first have the financial receipt canceled by the Registrar of the CBOT. This can be done during any business day. Then, during any business day, the holder of the financial receipt may surrender it at the office of the issuing vault or its correspondent bank as indicated on the financial receipt. Within 24 hours after surrender, the vault delivers the commercial paper to the party that presented the financial receipt.

How to trade

To bridge the gap between an academic environment and the players' circle, simulations of actual trades will now be presented. The examples are anecdotes so that basic procedures unique to commodity trading can also be reviewed. Practical applications have been selected for most interest rate contracts that are currently traded on regulated exchanges. In addition, an example of a bond trade is included in this chapter, since many readers may never have participated in such a transaction. Exhibits D, E, and F illustrate a trade confirmation, a purchase and sale report, and a monthly statement associated with a commodity trade.

BOND TRADING

On January 30, 1978, I. M. Sure asks a broker to select an appropriate bond investment that will produce income, safety and liquidity. The broker is aware of an upcoming government auction and recommends the purchase of ten Treasury bonds yielding 8.25 percent with a 15-year maturity. The following events depict the transaction:

Step 1:   I. M. Sure acknowledges the broker's recommendation to purchase ten 8.25's of 1993 for settlement in five business days after the bonds are issued.

Step 2:   Sure deposits a 10 percent ($1,000) margin with the broker and awaits the outcome of the auction.

Step 3:   Sure is notified by the broker on February 3, 1978, that the auction is completed. Sure bought ten bonds, each with a face value of $1,000, bearing an 8.25 percent coupon with a 15-year maturity at a price of 100.

Step 4:   I. M. Sure is invoiced for $10,000, which must be paid in five business days.

Step 5:   On February 5, Sure pays the remaining $9,000.

I. M. Sure now owns ten U.S. Treasury bonds that will pay 8.25 percent interest annually for 15 years. Interest payments are made semiannually and the principal will be repaid by the U.S. government in 15 years.

On August 1, 1978, I. M. Sure is suddenly confronted with an unforeseen expense and must liquidate this bond holding. Sure calls the broker and is advised that interest rate levels for this type of security recently have risen to 8.5 percent. The selling price now must be adjusted to reflect the higher yield level. The broker refers to a yield book and informs I. M. Sure that he will receive $972.50 for each bond sold. If on the day of sale, yield levels had fallen to 8 percent from 8.25 percent for 15-year Treasury bonds, Sure would have received $1,030 for each bond sold.

TRADING INTEREST RATE FUTURES

Commodity contracts for interest rate futures behave in the same manner as bonds and T-bills; when yields go down, prices go up.

Before N. O. Cash, our trader, can design a hedging strategy using interest rate futures, Cash must open a commodity account. This requires different customer agreements than those demanded for an equity account in which both stocks and bonds are traded. In addition, the broker may insist that the initial commodity transaction be accompanied by a $5,000 minimum balance. Once an account has been opened, commodity business can be conducted. Regardless of which contract is traded, it is essential that the customer become acquainted with the initial margin requirements of the member firm. The initial margin can be considered a security deposit, which guarantees the performance of a customer when a margin call is made. Margins and commissions may differ slightly among brokerage houses. They are also different for hedgers and speculators. These fees are normally so standard, however, that confidence in one's broker should determine the firm where business will be conducted. Ideally no more than 50 percent of the initial available balance should be absorbed by initial margin requirements. This will give N. O. Cash the ability to withstand temporary market reversals without being exposed to additional margin calls—the first commandment of commodity trading.

Once a trade is executed, a verbal confirmation is received and is followed by a written confirmation. Statements are mailed monthly to reflect current profits or losses. If a position is closed with an offsetting transaction, an invoice will be received that shows the available new balance after the results of the trade and commissions have been applied.

Although margin calls have been mentioned repeatedly, their trigger mechanisms have not been clarified. If the available balance of a speculative commodity account is reduced to a level below 80 percent of the required initial margin, an account representative contacts the customer by phone and asks that the available balance in the account be increased to the required initial margin level. This verbal notification is followed by a mailed margin notice (see Exhibit G). Computations are based on the previous night's closing prices. A margin call must be made even if prices have readjusted in favor of the customer by the time the contract begins trading the next morning. The customer is obliged to meet a margin call by mail or federal wire transfer. If a customer fails to respond within a reasonable amount of time, a position can be sold out, and any loss sustained is deducted from the available balance. If a contract has increased in value, the investor can withdraw the surplus balance above the initial margin amount by simply requesting a check or using the federal funds wire transfer system.

GNMA mortgage interest rate futures

Let us assume that on November 4, 1977, N. O. Cash decides to take a speculative position in the GNMA market because Cash believes long-term rates will soon increase. Therefore, N. O. Cash arbitrarily selects to sell one June 1978 contract at a price of 96-06. Yields increase, and on December 12, 1977, she buys back, or offsets, one June 1978 contract for 95-26. The steps illustrating this transaction are:

Step 1: Initial payment of $5,000 is made on October 30, 1977, or before the trade date. This deposit becomes the available balance.

Step 2: N. O. Cash sells one June 1978 contract on November 4 at 96-06. The available balance of $5,000 is reduced by $1,500, which is the current required speculative margin for one contract. The margin amount may change from time to time.

Step 3: Excess funds in the account are now reduced to $3,500.

Step 4: Excess funds are increased or decreased by the profits or losses generated by daily mark to market results. A margin call will be made if the available balance becomes less than 80 percent of the initial margin requirements.

Step 5: On December 12, 1977, Cash offsets the June 1978 contract at 95-26. This trade increases the available money balance of N. O. Cash by $31.25 $\times$ 12/32, or $375.00.

If Cash had sold the June 1978 contract in November and yields had gone down and prices up, a loss would have been sustained. If Cash had offset this position on November 27 at 96-26, the available balance in the account would have been reduced by $31.25 $\times$ 20/32, or $625.00.

Long-term government bonds

Encouraged by this profitable GNMA trade, N. O. Cash now decides to tackle the long-term government contract. Cash carefully studies available economic data, listens to business associates, reads *The Wall Street Journal,* and reviews several charts. Cash

130

arrives at the conclusion that long-term rates have temporarily topped out. This convinces her to buy, or go long, three September 1978 government bond contracts on January 5, 1978, at 94-16. On January 18, Cash is jubilant since yields dropped and prices closed at 95-06. On January 23, at 4:00 P.M., the OPEC countries decide to increase the price of oil by 20 percent. The next day the dollar comes under immense pressure in Zurich, and there are new forecasts of a more rapid rate of inflation than had been expected. By 11:00 A.M. on January 24, the government bond contracts fall their limit.[1] They open again on January 25 at 94-00, at which time N. O. Cash decides to sell out. This is a rather bleak scenerio, but one that could occur. Here is a chronological review of these events:

Step 1: On or before January 4, 1978, an initial payment of $5,000 is made. The account now has an available balance of $5,000.

Step 2: On January 5, N. O. Cash buys three September 1978 long-term government bond contracts at 94-16. The available balance is reduced by $4,500 based on the current speculator initial margin requirements of $1,500 per contract.

Step 3: Excess funds in the account are reduced to $500.

Step 4: As of January 18, excess funds have been increased or decreased by the results of daily mark to market activities. Cash's position has improved by $2,062.50, since September 1978 closed at 95-06 on January 18. This profit is generated by an increase in value of $31.25 × 22/32 for each open contract. Excess funds are now $2,562.50.

Step 5: On January 24, the contract drops its limit to 94-14, or $31.25 × 24/32, which is $750 per contract. Since N. O. Cash has three open positions, the excess funds are reduced by $2,250.00 to $312.50.

Step 6: On January 25, the market opens lower. Cash calls the broker and is informed that the September 1978 long-term government bonds are trading at 94-00. Cash quickly calculates the total loss to be $1,500, which re-

---

[1] Bond limit move in January 1978 was 24/32.

duces the available balance to $3,500, which is less than 80 percent of the required initial margin of $4,500. This means Cash will receive a margin call to bring the available balance back up to $4,500. Rather than conform to this request, Cash decides to sell out the position and close the account.

Step 7:   Cash instructs the broker to sell three September 1978 long-term government contracts at market. They are sold at 94-00. The total loss is $31.25 × 48/32, or $1,500.

Step 8:   Cash's available balance is reduced to $3,500. A check for that amount, less commissions, is mailed to N. O. Cash on January 25, 1978.

T-bills

C. Fast, a money market trader at a commercial bank has $1 million available for six months. Fast determines that a 90-day T-bill can be bought on the Chicago Mercantile Exchange for March 1977 delivery, on November 4, 1976, for 94.70, the equivalent of a 5.30 discount yield. Overnight federal funds are trading at 5.10 percent. On that date, a 26-week bill can be bought on the cash market at a 5.03 bank discount rate. Based on this relationship, Fast buys one March 1977 contract with the intention of standing for delivery, or offsetting the position shortly before the settlement date. Simultaneously the available cash is invested in overnight federal funds. This may be considered a substitute transaction, since it replaces or defers a cash market trade for a temporary period of time. The following steps describe the events of the trade:

Step 1:   Initial payment of $5,000 is made on or before November 1, 1976.

Step 2:   On November 4, Fast buys one March 1977 contract at 94.70. The available money balance is reduced by $1,000 since the customer represents a commercial bank and therefore is charged a hedge margin. This margin amount may vary from time to time.

Step 3:   The available balance is increased or decreased by a profit or loss as reflected by the daily mark to margin.

However, since C. Fast intends to take delivery of a T-bill in March, the cost of meeting a margin call is only coincidental to the transaction.

Step 4: By February 28, 1977, short-term rates have improved. Ninety-day T-bills are now selling at a 4.85 percent bank discount rate, or an IMM index of 95.15. The available balance in this account increases by 45 points. The value of that price fluctuation for this contract is $25 × 45, or $1,125. C. Fast decides to offset his position.

Step 5: On March 1, 1977, at 10:30 A.M., Fast instructs the broker to sell one March 1977 T-bill contract at the market, and close his account.

Step 6: On March 1, 1977, at 11 A.M., the broker confirms the sale of one March 1977 T-bill contract at 95.10. The $1,000 profit and the initial $5,000, less commission, are returned to C. Fast. On the same day Fast purchases a $1 million T-bill for next-day settlement in the cash market at a yield of 4.82 percent. In effect, the substitute transaction on the Merc enables Fast to buy a T-bill at a 5.30 percent discount rate on March 1, 1977 while investing immediate funds in federal funds until March 1, 1977.

Commercial paper

S.S. is the treasurer of a major toy corporation, which sells commercial paper in the fall to meet its seasonal cash requirements. During the summer of 1978, 90-day A-1 commercial paper rates are approximately 7.75 and economists are projecting higher rates for the rest of the year. Based on corporate cash flow projections, S.S. hopes to lock in the approximate current rates for the company's fall borrowing needs of $10 million.

This is done on June 19, 1978, when S.S. calls a commodity broker and buys ten December 1978 commercial paper loan contracts at a price of 8.90. The following steps describe the procedure and the results of the hedge program.

Step 1: On June 15, 1978, S.S. opens a hedge commodity account for the Smasher Toy Company. An initial margin deposit of $12,000 is made. The toy company's available balance is now $12,000.

Step 2: On June 19, 1978, S.S. instructs the broker to buy ten December 1978 commercial paper loan contracts at 8.90 percent. December is selected because it most closely matches the time when the company expects to sell its commercial paper. This transaction reduces the available balance of the Smasher Toy Company by $10,000.

Step 3: Commercial paper rates continue to rise throughout the fall of 1978. On October 17, 1978, S.S. offsets the ten December 1978 contracts at 9.64 percent and simultaneously sells $10 million of 90-day commercial paper at 9.00 percent through an investment banking firm. The Smasher Toy Company earns 74 basis points × $25 × 10. The total profit from this transaction is $18,500, less commissions.

Step 4: On October 18, 1978, a check for $29,900 is sent to the toy company. This amount represents the return of the $12,000 initial margin deposit, plus the profit from this transaction, less $600 commission.

Step 5: The hedging profit of $18,500 partially offsets the additional borrowing expense of $31,250 expended by the Smasher Toy Company when S.S. sells 90-day commercial paper on October 17, 1978. On that date, 90-day A-1 commercial paper is selling at 9.00 percent instead of the 7.75 percent available on June 19, 1978. Table 8-1 summarizes the transactions.

Table 8-1
Long hedge by commercial paper issuer

Cash market	Futures market
June 19	**June 19**
Wants to lock in a 7.75 percent rate on $10 million of 90-day commercial paper	Buys ten December 1978 commercial paper loan futures contracts at 8.90 percent
October 17	**October 17**
Issues $10 million of 90-day paper at 9.00 percent	Sells ten December 1978 contracts at 9.64 percent
Increased borrowing cost	**Gain**
$10,000,000 \times 1.25\% \times \dfrac{90}{360} = \$31,250$	74 basis points × $25 × 10 = $18,500

As a result of this strategy, the Smasher Toy Company is able to hold its commercial paper borrowing costs to an approximate rate of 8.28 percent, instead of the 9.00 percent that is in effect on October 17, 1978. If 90-day commercial paper rates had improved during this period of time, the corporation would have incurred a loss from the future hedge transaction. However, Smasher would have sold its commercial paper at a market rate lower than 7.75 percent. This would have enabled it to maintain a net borrowing cost of approximately 7.75 percent, which is deemed satisfactory for the profit plan. This hedge position effectively guaranteed the company's approximate borrowing rate on June 19, 1978, for the fall requirements.

SPREADS AND STRADDLES

Spreads, sometimes called *straddles,* are defined as the simultaneous purchase and sale of a fixed income security and a similar commodity interest rate contract, or two interest rate commodity contracts, for the purpose of generating a profit when the price relationships of these positions are readjusted to normal historical price spreads. A bond trader calls this type of trading *arbitrage.* It is done when two different securities appear to have a temporary pricing discrepancy. When their price relationships return to normal, both transactions are simultaneously offset. Either side of such a spread or straddle is called a *leg.* On some occasions, one leg may be lifted, or offset, at a time.

Since spread price movements are generally less volatile than absolute price movements, an initial margin for spreads is significantly lower than the margin associated with long or short positions. Some brokerage houses require that spread positions be marked to market only on a daily basis.

The most frequently used spread is called an *interdelivery spread,* or the simultaneous buying and selling of two different months of one commodity. A spread can be positioned between two GNMA contracts if a speculator detects an abnormal price relationship.

A second type of spread is called an *intercommodity spread,* or cross hedge. One commodity is sold while another is bought for

135

the same delivery month. On the CBOT market, the most famous intercommodity spread is called *crush spread* and is associated with soybean and soybean oil contracts. In financial markets, a spread between T-bills and long-term government contracts is a comparable example, since it can be used to offset the movements of a yield curve.

If a trader expects rapidly increasing short-term rates, he or she might consider selling T-bills and buying long-term government bond contracts with identical delivery dates. If the trader is correct, the T-bill contract will have a greater dollar move than the long-term government position although the maturities and face amounts of the contracts differ greatly. This is also an example of an *intermarket spread*, since the T-bill contract is traded on the Merc and the long-term government contract is traded on the CBOT.

Without special arrangements between the clearing corporations of both exchanges, such a spread would probably be inefficient, since the spread trader could not obtain the advantage of lower initial spread margins. Special intermarket spread margin relationships are limited to commodities that have extremely good correlations and economic relationships. Currently, several interest rate contracts have been approved for this special consideration.

The intercommodity trade

T.M.S. closely observes and charts both the GNMA and the long-term government contracts. T.M.S. notes that the prices of similar expiration months have recently been 14/32 apart. On March 17, GNMAs appear temporarily overpriced, since thrift institutions are active buyers because of temporarily depressed mortgage originations.

T.M.S. decides to sell GNMAs and buy long-term governments with the expectation that their normal spread relationships will soon return.

136

Step 1: On March 1, 1978 T.M.S. deposits $5,000. The available balance is now $5,000.

Step 2: On March 17, T.M.S. buys one June 1978 long-term government contract at 96-10 and sells one June 1978 GNMA contract at 97-00. This reduces the balance by $750, which is the speculative initial margin for a spread transaction.

Step 3: Excess funds are now reduced to $4,250.

Step 4: On May 16, the spread between these contracts has returned to near normal, as GNMA yields have increased more rapidly than long-term government yields. T.M.S. sells one June 1978 long-term government contract at 96-02 and buys one June 1978 GNMA contract at 96-18.

Step 5: The net profit of 6/32 from this transaction is computed as follows:

Date	GNMA		Long-term government	
March 17	Sold	97-00	Bought	96-10
May 16	Bought	96-18	Sold	96-02
		+14		−08

Step 6: T.M.S.'s funds are credited with $31.25 × 6, or $187.50.

Step 7: T.M.S. withdraws the available balance and obtains a check for $5,187.50, less commissions. Commissions are also lower for spreads than they are for two separate transactions.

This trade exemplifies an intercommodity trade that performed satisfactorily. The results from such cross-hedge applications are usually less predictable and more volatile than other hedging transactions. This type of trade must be watched continually, since its correlation may change due to various outside influences.

Mortgage banking applications

THE MORTGAGE BANKING INDUSTRY

For one who enjoys selling, second guessing money markets, and managing highly leveraged institutions staffed by motivated individuals, the profession of mortgage banking can be extremely rewarding. Its members continually risk their capital by making mortgage investments tied to long-term rates while financing their operation with short-term funds.

The mortgage banking industry's roots can be traced to 1914, when 45 real estate lenders founded the Farm Mortgage Bankers Association of America.[1] They specifically excluded brokers and corporations that specialized in financing metropolitan housing. They offered investors an "exceptionally reliable security" that was diligently guarded until maturity. The average loan to value was less than 60 percent and the notes had a five-year nonamortiz-

---

[1] *Mortgage Banker*, October 1973.

ing term. The association enjoyed a great measure of success during the first decade of its existence. In the late 1920s, however, its membership recognized the need to diversify its lending practices and renamed itself the Mortgage Bankers Association (MBA). Urban lending became acceptable, as agricultural loans suffered from the effects of the depression. The creation of the Home Owner's Loan Corporation in 1933 and the Federal Housing Administration in 1934 added new dimensions to lending activities as mortgages began to be amortized, and permanent investors began to buy loans primarily based on their government guarantees.

By 1940 the size of the MBA had increased to more than 600 regular members. Significant income was generated from servicing loans that were located outside a permanent investor's normal lending area. Today, this source of funds represents from 30 to 40 percent of a mortgage company's annual income. This can be considered an annuity, since loan servicing generates an income stream until a loan is extinguished by a payoff or foreclosure.

A second important source of income for a mortgage company is the origination fees generated from the 1 percent closing fee that typically is associated with the initial mortgage balance of insured loans. Perhaps it can be called an administrative processing fee. Currently, direct and indirect expenses related to selling and closing activities exceed this fee if the loan is less than $60,000. Therefore, marketing profits generated from originations become a critical ingredient if a mortgage banker wishes to earn reasonable profit margins. Since the stockholders' equity of a typical mortgage company averaged 10 percent of assets in 1977, it is not difficult to realize that such leverage is an asset in a market with improving interest rates but devastating in a rising market. The need to hedge production is critical to the long-term well-being of this industry. One way of hedging is to knowledgeably use the interest rate futures market.

The word *knowledgeable* is carefully selected because interest rate futures contracts do not replace other marketing tools available to the mortgage originator. Futures should be used as a supplement to other hedging techniques when and where appropriate.

140

HEDGING INSURED LOANS WITH GNMA FUTURES

The production cycle, or origination cycle as it is sometimes called, can be analyzed by segregating mortgage applications into new construction and existing loan categories.[2] Normally refinancing applications require 60 to 90 days from the time an application is taken until the loan is closed. This represents a risk to the originator since industry pressures often require the issuing of a firm 90-day commitment letter based on the price in existence when the application is taken. Therefore, if the originator does not sell the loan or hedge these commitments immediately, the company can be exposed to a sizable loss. Builder loans carry less risk than spot loans if they are negotiated to close at market rates or have a front-end fee associated with a specific commitment. A 1 percent change in residential mortgage interest rate levels (100 BP) for a 30-year mortgage, priced at an average life of twelve years, causes an approximate price change of 7.5 points,[3] or $75 per $1,000 mortgage balance. Thus a change of 10 BP, which is not uncommon occurrence during a 90-day period, might affect the price of 9 percent conventional mortgage by 32/32, or $7,000 per $1 million face value. If we multiply this potential loss by 100 to simulate the annual origination volume of a medium-size mortgage company, the exposure would seriously damage a corporation's profitability and cash flow.

Before selecting a GNMA interest rate futures contract as a hedging vehicle against production, the marketing department of the originating organization should examine the following alternatives:

1. Selling whole loans to a private investor.
2. Participating in the FNMA auction.
3. Selling a GNMA security.

If whole loan commitments are momentarily unavailable, or their terms are unsatisfactory, and the FNMA auction is not scheduled

---

[2] This is a refinancing transaction usually associated with an existing property.

[3] Represents a purchase price in terms of a percentage of par value. Seven points are the equivalent of 93 percent of par.

for another ten days, a comparison between selling GNMA futures and GNMA securities is in order (see Table 9-1).

Table 9-1
GNMA futures versus securities

	GNMA mortgage-backed securities	GNMA mortgage interest rate futures
Dollar amount . .	Usually quoted in $1 million	$100,000 per contract
Liquidity	Depends on GNMA dealers' inventory	Check open contracts for month selected
Time frame	30-180 days	30 months
Cost to buy and sell	4/32	$60 per contract, or negotiated rate
Margin	Per dealer policy*	$1,000 per contract for hedgers and daily mark to market calls
Pricing	Per-dealer quote	Centralized open outcry; price displayed on inquiry screen
Security of transaction . . .	As good as dealer	Backed by dealer, regulated exchange, and clearing corporation
Delivery	Can be offset by buy-back	Can be offset by buy-back
FHA rate	Bought or sold for a specific coupon, but has yield maintainance capabilities with par stop	Differs with selected contract, generally insensitive to a contract rate change

*This concept is continually examined by regulatory agencies.

The successful short hedge against mortgage production

If interest rate futures still appear to be an attractive alternative for the marketing manager of the Unbelievable Mortgage Company, the following analysis must be made:

1. Compare and analyze the yield spreads between available GNMA premium and discount coupons in the cash market. Select the cheapest readily available security for making an IVT test; this will be the coupon associated with the greatest yield. If premium securities are trading at yields equal to those of discount bonds, or are unavailable, make the IVT analysis using the currently traded coupon.

142

2. Compute the IVT as described in Chapter 4.
3. Test the price levels of the back month as discussed in Chapter 4.

For this exercise let us assume it is 1:00 P.M. on March 28, 1977, and the following economic conditions and prices are reported:

1. Immediate cash GNMA prices and yields.

Coupons	Price	Yield
9	105-15	8.20
8	99-06	8.06

2. CBOT prices at 1:00 P.M. on March 28, 1977.

Contract month	Price
June 1977	97.07
September 1977	96.00
December 1977	95.06

3. Miscellaneous spread analysis.
    a. The yield spread between GNMA 8's and 9's is 14 BP. These coupons appear to have a valid relationship.
    b. The yield spread between 90-day T-bills and Treasury bonds is 200 BP.
    c. The yield spread between GNMAs and Treasury bonds is 30 BP.
4. Additional economic observations.
    a. The yield curve is wide but is expected to flatten by 25 BP during the next three months and remain at this new level for the next 180 days.
    b. Long-term rates appear steady. Both the Consumer Price Index and the Wholesale Price Index appear under control.
    c. Housing demand continues strong, but the savings inflow to thrift institutions remains strong.
    d. The FNMA auction receives little attention since most production is sold as a GNMA security.

From this information the marketing staff of the Unbelievable Mortgage Company should expect the yield curve to remain at its approximate current position. If it begins to flatten, the spread between the back contracts could start to narrow. This narrowing effect, in addition to the normal price convergence, would be detrimental to a short position in the back months. Therefore, if the front month can be used for shorting at this time, it would be preferable. To determine the current contract price levels in relationship to the cash market, an IVT must be performed. Following the IVT procedures defined in Chapter 4, the following calculations are made using the data given above.

Step 1:   105-15
Step 2:   105.468
Step 3:   105.468 × 0.931 = 98.19
Step 4:   98-06
Step 5:   Add 30/32 to the nearby GNMA interest rate futures contract. For this exercise the nearby month is June 1977, quoted at 97-07. When 30/32, the convergence factor, is added to the price of 97-07, the result is 98-05.
Step 6:   Adjusted September price is 98-05; the 8's equivalent price from Step 4 is 98-06.

In conclusion, the adjusted nearby contract is priced 2/32 under the immediate 8's equivalent price. Therefore, it can be used to short, although a zero or plus spread would be more desirable.

The September 1977 contract is also suitable for shorting since the June-September 1977 spread relationship appears normal based on current interest rates. As previously stated, the second or third contract month of an interest rate futures contract is more reliable for shorting, since nearby months can occasionally come under unusual price pressures as a settlement date approaches or a GNMA coupon rate change is anticipated.

Since the yield curve is not expected to flatten significantly and the second contract month appears properly priced for shorting, the September 1977 contract is selected to hedge mortgage production on March 28, 1977. After 30 days, the results are very satisfactory, as shown in the accompanying table. In analyzing this hedge example, it must be remembered that both the forward cash and the futures market experience convergence.

Date	GNMA cash market 8's prices for immediate delivery	GNMA September 1977 contract prices
March 28, 1977	99-06	96-03
April 28, 1977	99-16	96-22
	+10/32	+19/32

This particular correlation is very satisfactory. In this exercise, 10/32 per month was used for convergence, which is also known as *backwardation.*[4] The factor used is based on the short- to long-term yield spread in effect on March 28, 1977. Table 4-5 was used to compute this monthly convergence factor. Therefore, the futures price increase of 19/32 approximates the sum of the change in the immediate cash market plus the effect of one month's backwardation during April 1977.

In summary, a successful hedger must be alert to:

1. The degree and change in, direction of the long-term Treasury bond yield level in existence while a hedge is in place. This will affect the yield spread between discount and premium bonds and the basis between cash and futures.
2. Watch the yield curve. If it shifts, it can be dynamite. Flattening favors the long position in the back contracts.
3. The appropriate futures contract must be selected before the hedger takes either a long or short position. There are times when it is inappropriate to short or go long. Perhaps a partial hedge could be the solution to a problem during such periods.

If any of these factors changes rapidly while a hedge is in place, be ready to alter your hedge plan. Do not be afraid to reduce or increase your position, roll over a position to another contract month, or offset your position entirely. A strategy must be flexible, relatively cheap to administer, and insensitive to FHA rates, and it must optimize profits or minimize losses. Above all, it should be in written form.

---

[4] See Pricing GNMA Cash Forward Market Securities in Chapter 4 and glossary in Chapter 3.

Improper short hedging against mortgage production

A successful marketing manager of today requires more knowledge than his or her predecessors. It is no longer sufficient to understand the FNMA auction and regularly visit with major eastern investors. Now the manager must also understand sectors of the government bond market in order to evaluate the relative price levels of GNMA securities and be conversant in interest rate futures markets. In addition the manager must still maintain a relationship with whole loan buyers. Once these skills are mastered, managers will be able to avoid the type of mousetrap that was sprung on some mortgage bankers and account representatives who placed a short GNMA hedge against production during January 1977 using the GNMA interest rate contract.

The market was in a bull cycle with GNMA prices improving rapidly throughout the last quarter of 1976. The FHA contract rate was expected to be reduced momentarily from 8.5 to 8 percent. The outlook for long-term rates, as reflected by most economists, continued to be rosy. There were rumbles that short-term rates might go up slowly but long-term rates would continue at their current levels. However, there was one significant aberration in the mortgage market. GNMA 7.5's and 8's were trading outside their historical price relationships in the cash market. GNMA 9's appeared properly priced in relationship to the cash 8's. On January 4, 1977, 7.5's were priced at 100-02 and 8's were at 102-10. Their normal price spread relationship at the current yield level had been about 3-15 for the past year. To the professional, arbitrage opportunities seemed obvious. Judging from historical yield spread relationships, the 7.5's were much too expensive compared with the other coupons. It was evident that if the market were to sell off, the 7.5's would be exposed to significant losses. In January 1977, the bond market broke and that is exactly what happened. By March 2, the cash market had corrected itself. The FHA contract rate had also been lowered to 8 percent and current production was going into GNMA 7.5 percent securities. The spread between the 7.5's and 8's had widened from 2-08 in January to 3-12 in March.

An examination of the results of a short futures hedge placed by the Unbelievable Mortgage Company against production on January 4, 1977 reveals the following: The hedge was properly placed but improperly designed. It was impossible to hedge GNMA 7.5's with futures on a dollar for dollar basis at that time, since they were uniquely overpriced.

On January 4, 1977, the following quotations were available for immediate cash bid prices and yields.

Coupons	Price	GNMA yield
9	108-15	7.85
8	102-10	7.64
7.5	100-02	7.45

The CBOT futures prices on January 4, 1977, were:

Date	Price
March 1977	100-14
June 1977	99-16
September 1977	98-18

The IVT generates the following steps:

Step 1: 108-15
Step 2: 108.47
Step 3: 108.47 X 0.931 = 100.98
Step 4: 100-31
Step 5: Add 24/32 to 100-14 based on Table 4-5.
Step 6: Compare the 8's equivalent price of 100-31 to the adjusted nearby futures price of 101-06.

In conclusion, the IVT indicates the nearby contract could be shorted on January 4, 1977. The back month price analysis discussed in Chapter 4 also concluded that the second and third options also could be used to short on January 4, 1977.

The results of the hedging program, which was designed to protect current production by shorting GNMA futures using either the March 1977 or June 1977 contract, were disturbing. For purposes of analysis, the positions were offset on March 2, 1977.

Obviously the correlation was unsatisfactory. An autopsy disclosed that the GNMA 7.5's rapidly corrected their yield relationships with other coupons during this time. When arbitrage trading pressures were superimposed on these corrections during a bear market, the results were unsatisfactory.

When the smoke cleared, some traders used this experience as proof that the GNMA futures market is unreliable and should not be used to hedge currently insured production. The facts speak for themselves; the fault was not the behavior of the contract, but the lack of foresight on the part of the hedge planners. A realization that unique cash market relationships existed on January 4 could have predicted the outcome. GNMA interest rate futures contracts, which do not permit delivery of GNMA securities at prices above par, would probably have produced far better results.[5] In addition, we must also recognize that a premium bond is a cushion bond in a bear market. Premium bonds give up less value than discount bonds during such times. This would account for the imprecise correlation between the cash 8's and the futures contracts during this period.

Table 9-2

		March 1977	June 1977
Prices of GNMA futures contracts			
Sold	January 4, 1977	100-14	99-16
Bought	March 2, 1977	97-20	96-16
	Difference	2-24	3-00
Prices of GNMA cash securities		7.5's	8's
Sold	January 4, 1977	100-02	102-10
Bought	March 2, 1977	95-23	99-03
	Difference	4-11	3-07

FHA/VA hedging summary

Soundly placed short hedges have performed satisfactorily. Throughout 1978, the interest rate futures markets provided satis-

---

[5] The CBOT and ACE direct certificate delivery contracts began trading in September 1978.

factory hedging protection for production. When contract price levels and economic factors are favorable for shorting, such action is recommended. A mortgage originator may not always wish to hedge dollar for dollar. A partial hedging program could be selectively developed to permit putting on or taking off contracts equal to 25 to 100 percent of production. It is noteworthy that interest rate futures contracts have no pricing penalty for adding or deleting one contract instead of ten. Therefore, the contracts can also be used to protect the value of temporarily uninsured loans in inventory.

STANDBYS

The money managers' comfort blanket is an inactive interest rate market. This phenomenon disappeared with the Packard, Nash, and Hudson automobiles. It is now normal to have mortgage yield levels, as defined by GNMA cash prices, FNMA auction results, or the FHLMC's average weekly conventional price index, fluctuate 5 to 20 percent in one year. If the Unbelievable Mortgage Company originates $100 million of loans in a 12-month period, it could experience a marketing loss of $300,000 to $500,000 if it does not prudently presell production. To illustrate this exposure, examine Table 9-3, which displays the price effect of yield level changes for specific GNMA coupons.

This magnitude of loss is unacceptable to the average mortgage company. Preventive measures for a mortgage originator might include the purchase of standbys. These are synonymous with puts

Table 9-3
Percentage GNMA price change as a result of yield change

Annual GNMA yield levels		Yield change (per-cent)	GNMA price change by coupon							
			8's				9's			
High	Low		High	Low	Differ-ence	Per-cent	High	Low	Differ-ence	Per-cent
9.75	8.50	14.70	87-29	96-03	8-06	8.5	94-17	103-08	8-23	8.4
8.10	7.25	11.72	98-30	105-12	6-12	6.0	106-08	113-01	6-25	6.0
8.60	8.20	4.87	95-13	98-07	2-26	2.8	102-16	105-15	2-31	2.8

in the equity market. They are purchased by a mortgage originator for a nonrecoverable fee, which is earned by a standby writer. Usually the writer is a permanent investor willing to fund loans at a predetermined time for a predetermined price that is less than current market levels. Under controlled conditions, the interest rate futures market can be used by a buyer to attempt to recover this fee by going long in a carefully selected GNMA futures contract month. Before analyzing a fundamental formula pertaining to this application, a discussion of the logic associated with the standby concept is appropriate.

Mortgage originators who do not have the assurance that permanent funds will always be available to them must consider the purchase of a standby commitment as a normal cost of doing business. The dollar amount of standbys purchased is a function of company policy. It probably varies with interest rate projections. A prudent originator will maintain a minimal amount of standby coverage at all times to protect the company against rapidly rising interest rates.

During such times a marketing manager may select to deliver loans against previously purchased standbys whose strike prices may now be more favorable than current cash market quotations. To implement this procedure, the marketing manager notifies the writer of the standby of his intention to deliver in accordance with a tailored standby agreement that was signed by the mortgage banker and the permanent investor when the agreement was negotiated. Since these contracts are usually written for 6, 12, or 24 months, they offer unusual opportunities for both parties. At select times, GNMA interest rate futures contracts can be used to recover all or a portion of a standby fee paid to obtain these long-term commitments.

The most significant hypothesis associated with this concept assumes that the price of the nearby futures month merges with the immediate GNMA bid price in the cash market on the expiration date of the futures contract. Therefore, for this application it is important to select a futures contract month whose expiration date closely follows the expiration date of the standby commitment.

150

Secondly, it is assumed that the price behavior of the futures contract will have a close correlation to the price behavior of the cheapest available GNMA security. When available, this is usually a premium coupon. When all available coupons trade at the same yield levels, the futures contract price should merge with the currently traded coupon.

During periods when futures contracts trade off premium securities, the basis between the contract and the GNMA cash market depends on the yield spreads between the least expensive security and the currently traded GNMA security. As can be seen in Table 4-10, the nearby futures market does not expire with a constant basis relationship to cash. As the yield levels of Treasury bonds increase, the spread narrows between discount and premium bonds with similar maturities. When yield levels are relatively low, the nearby futures contract may close out at one point, or 32/32 below the cash price. As Treasury bond yield levels increase, this spread may be narrowed to 16/32. The June 1978 contract closed out precisely at the immediate cash GNMA price.

Since the futures market can be used to obtain delivery of a GNMA security that can be redelivered against a cash market GNMA obligation, it is not probable that either market will drift too far from the other for too long before arbitrage corrects the distortion.

If a GNMA futures contract that expires simultaneously with the GNMA cash standby commitment can be purchased below the net standby strike price, less a variable which reflects the spread between the cheapest available GNMA coupon and the current production coupon all or a portion of the nonrecoverable standby fee often can be recovered. For this study 16/32 is used since the fraction is representative of the existing spread during the second quarter of 1978.

Profit indicator for standby cross hedge

It is not always possible to find a GNMA interest rate futures contract that is properly priced to activate this application. Opportunities generally occur when market psychology has driven the back months to an unusually pessimistic price level or when the yield curve is very steep. When this occurs, the estimated profit or loss generated from such a transaction can be computed as follows:

$$\binom{\text{Profit}}{\text{indicator}} = \binom{\text{Net standby strike price for an}}{\text{equivalent 8 percent GNMA}} - \binom{\text{Price of selected}}{\text{futures contract}} + 16/32^{*}$$

*This fraction changes in relationship to the yield spread between the cheapest available GNMA coupon and the current coupon.

If the profit indicator is positive, recovery of the fee is likely. If the profit indicator is a negative number the strategy should not be pursued. The ability to achieve this objective will vary when:

1. Futures are offset before or after the standby commitment is executed.
2. The basis between premium and discount bonds changes more than 16/32 between the time the position is executed and when it is offset.
3. The interest rate futures market loses its correlation to the cash market.
4. Yield curve becomes inverted.

Cross hedging a standby fee

To illustrate the result of this application in improving, neutral, and down markets, consider the following scenario.

Given. On June 15, 1978, the immediate bid price for an 8.5 percent GNMA is 95-29. The June 1979 contract is priced at 88-26. A standby commitment is purchased by a mortgage originator with the following conditions:

Term:	1 year, 30-day notice
Amount:	$1 million GNMA security, ±2.5 percent
Strike price:	For 8.5's, 93-28
Fee:	1.25 points, nonrecoverable
Other:	Par stop with yield maintenance
Net cost of standby to buyer:	92-20, 8's equivalent price 89-09.

Profit indicator test

$$
\begin{aligned}
\text{Profit indicator} &= (89\text{-}09/32) - (88\text{-}26/32 + 16/32) \\
&= (89\text{-}09/32) - (89\text{-}10/32) \\
&= (-1/32) = \text{neutral signal}
\end{aligned}
$$

The marketing manager decides to buy the available June 1979 standby and simultaneously go long ten June 1979 GNMA mortgage interest rate futures contracts.

Assume market improves. The mortgage originator will not execute the standby unless the immediate GNMA cash market falls below 93-28 for GNMA 8.5's. Therefore, the nonrefundable fee of 1.25 points is lost. However, the futures contract will increase in value due to improving market conditions and convergence. The result is that profit from the futures contract can be used to offset the expense of purchasing a standby fee.

Assume market remains neutral. The mortgage originator will not execute the standby unless the immediate GNMA cash market falls below 93-28 for GNMA 8.5's. Therefore, the nonrefundable fee is lost again. The long futures position can be expected to increase in price during the one-year period by the approximate spread that separates the September 1979 contract from the September 1978 contract at the time the position is executed. Variations from this estimate can occur. They would be a function of yield levels or changes in the slope of the existing yield curve at the time the contract is offset. The result is that the profit generated from the convergence of the futures contract can be used to offset expended standby fees.

Assume market deteriorates. The mortgage originator will deliver against a standby if the immediate price drops below 93-28 for GNMA 8.5's. Delivery can occur in two ways. The most common procedure is to allocate a portion of the current production against the standby commitment. In that way mortgages that close at market rates below the strike price can be delivered at a profit for payment at 93-28. In addition, the owner of a standby has the option of purchasing a GNMA security in the cash market and redelivering it against the commitment. In either case, the gross profit is a function of the acquisition price. As previously stated, this gross profit must be reduced by the standby fee to arrive at a net profit or loss for this transaction.

If the market is in a pronounced downward trend, maintaining a long position in an interest rate futures contract will negate the primary justification for having purchased the standby. The usual reason for such a purchase is to provide the organization with a floor price during a down market for a specific amount of production. Although a long position held open until a standby is exercised probably will not produce a net loss, it will undoubtedly eliminate any chance for generating a net profit from the standby commitment. Therefore, it is recommended that a "stop loss" be placed 24/32 or one point below the price at which the long futures position is exercised. If the stop loss is triggered, the originator will incur an additional expense, which should be added to the cost of acquiring a standby. However, the owner of a standby then can have the opportunity to generate income from such a commitment. This profit can be used to offset marketing losses that are generally incurred by an originator in a bear interest rate market.

The risk related to such a strategy could be a rapid reversal of interest rate trends occurring shortly after a stop loss is triggered. Since market trends are generally sawtoothed in directions, this risk can be minimized or maximized only by enlarging or decreasing the stop loss levels.

If a stop loss order is not placed in a bear market and the long position remains open until the standby is executed, the originator will deliver against the standby, offset the long position, and probably generate a zero net profit from the standby commitment. In addition, margin funds must be maintained throughout a bear cycle if the long futures position is not offset. The following results are illustrative of such a transaction. The price levels on June 15, 1979, are hypothetical.

On June 15, 1979, the immediate price for an 8.5 percent GNMA is 91-06, reflecting a yield of 9.753. The originator delivers against the standby at a price of 93-28 and earns a gross profit of $25,625 per million. The gross profit is reduced by the $12,500 standby fee, thus generating a net profit of $13,125.

At a 9.75 percent yield level, it is assumed that there are no premium GNMA bonds outstanding and that the futures market is closely tracking a current 9.25 percent coupon. At this yield level, a GNMA 8 percent security will be priced at 87-28. Since we assume that the futures contract will go off the board 16/32 below cash, we can estimate a closing price of 87-12 on June 15, 1979, for the June 1979 contract. In this event, the originator would have a futures loss of 46/32, or $14,375. This would approximately offset the net marketing profit generated by delivering a GNMA security for payment at 93-28 during June 1979, which was purchased in the immediate cash market or assembled from current mortgage production. This projection will become invalid if the yield curve becomes flat or inverted.

CROSS HEDGING A FNMA BID

There are times when an approved FNMA servicer becomes acutely aware of the importance of the next FNMA auction. When the originator has been unable to obtain the necessary whole loan commitments to cover production, and when the GNMA cash prices appear unreasonable, the upcoming FNMA auction becomes significant.

Before entering a bid, a servicer carefully analyzes available data from past FNMA auctions, the GNMA cash market, and the price levels of selected government bonds. A bid can then be submitted by a servicer for a dollar amount before 1:00 P.M. EDT every second Monday of a month. The bidder will know whether a bid is successful by comparing his or her submission with the accepted price levels, which are publicly released the next afternoon. Written acknowledgments are received from FNMA the following day.

Since the range for successful bids can be ±1.5 points, or $15 per $1,000, it can be significant if the bidder is successful by submitting a bid that is in the acceptable high range. To accomplish this on repeated occasions, a servicer must avoid unreasonable self-imposed pressures. One way of reducing these pressures in an active bear market is to short a futures contract on the Monday on which bids are submitted. If the bid is accepted on Tuesday, the futures positions should be offset. If the bid is rejected, the short position can be maintained until the next auction. Table 9-4 lists the insured FNMA auction results between April 17, 1978, and June 12, 1978, when the bond market was in the midst of a severe retraction.

Table 9-4
FNMA insured auction results

Date	Dollar amount bid/accepted ($ millions)	Average yield	Average price	Price range
6/12/78	522/285	9.862	94.22	92.06-94.44
5/30/78	851/447	9.827	94.44	93.59-94.70
5/15/78	611/297	9.625	94.08	91.06-94.19
5/01/78	655/350	9.524	94.74	94.00-94.85
4/17/78	283/165	9.437	95.31	94.01-95.51

To test the results of this application, assume that an IVT is made for the September 1978 contract on each day the mortgage originator submits a bid. The IVT results confirm that the contract can be used for shorting at that moment. The hedge results for two alternatives are depicted as follows:

1. Alternative A: The short position is offset on the following day when the bidder is informed that his bid is accepted (see Table 9-5).
2. Alternative B: The bidder is unsuccessful in his attempt to obtain FNMA coverage. The short position now is offset on the date of the next auction (see Table 9-6).

The simulated results are not conclusive and do not include commissions and costs associated with margins. They do reflect the correlation between the FNMA auction and GNMA futures markets during this specific time period.

156

Table 9-5
Alternative A: Bid accepted and position offset the next day

Date short position taken	Cash bid price for GNMA 8.25's at 2:30 P.M. EDT	September 1978 GNMA futures prices at 2:30 P.M. EDT
April 17	96-19	93-10
April 18	96-19	93-07
Net change	0	−03
May 1	95-18	92-19
May 2	95-17	92-18
Net change	−01	−01
May 15	95-10	91-31
May 16	95-12	92-01
Net change	+02	+02
May 31	94-02	90-23
June 1	94-04	90-25
Net change	+02	+02
June 12	94-08	91-00
June 13	94-07	90-30
Net change	−01	−02

Table 9-6
Alternative B: Bid rejected, trader maintains short
position until next auction

Date short position taken	Cash bid price for GNMA 8.25's at 2:30 P.M. EDT	September 1978 GNMA futures prices at 2:30 P.M. EDT
April 18	96-19	93-07
May 2	95-17	92-18
Net change	−34	−21
May 2	95-17	92-18
May 16	95-12	92-01
Net change	−05	−17
May 16	95-12	92-01
June 1	94-04	90-25
Net change	−40	−39
June 1	94-04	90-25
June 13	94-07	90-30
Net change	+03	+05

It can be seen that during this randomly selected two-month period, the bidder enjoyed an almost perfect correlation. Only once, on April 18, was the correlation poor. Although the deviation was in favor of the short hedger, it shows vividly that at any given moment the correlation between cash and futures may be imperfect. In the past, the price variance between GNMA cash and futures has been as great as 24/32' However, this occurred when the cash market basis between coupons was also imperfect. Generally a ±8/32 variation must be considered acceptable at any given moment.

Due to the effects of convergence, the futures contract should generally outperform the immediate cash market on the upside and lag the cash market on the downside. During this two-month period, all but the May 2 to May 16 results can be considered satisfactory. During this time, the futures contract exhibited an unsatisfactory correlation to cash. It is probable that the IVT performed on May 2 would have indicated a favorable signal for a short position, since the contract lagged the cash market during the prior two weeks.

In summation, this application should not be construed as a hedging vehicle. Rather, it is a creative example of utilizing interest rate futures. It is an example of a cross hedge for which the results are less predictable than for other hedges using identical securities. An analysis of how this contract can be used to cross hedge the Federal Home Loan Mortgage Corporation's participation certificate auction is given in Chapter 10.

Chapter
10

Investor applications

Anyone responsible for managing assets or liabilities for a thrift institution, commercial bank, pension fund, insurance company, or credit union must be keenly aware of continued profit pressures. In the past, these pressures often have occurred as a result of disintermediation. The development of the six-month money market certificates in the spring of 1978 reduced the problems of disintermediation at the expense of eroding interest rate breakage. This pinch was especially severe for savings and loan associations and mutual savings banks. Commercial banks confronted with similar challenges found it easier to generate high-yield income from commercial and installment loans. These problems are neither resolved nor avoided by the prudent use of interest rate futures. However, the continued existence of profit margin pressures should stimulate an examination of their possible usefulness to investment officers.

Before delving into specific applications, a review of the regulations that guide institutions in the use of these contracts is appropriate. Both the Comptroller of the Currency and the Federal Home Loan Bank Board have issued regulations outlining the acceptable uses of interest rate futures. State regulatory bodies generally have been silent on this issue.

REGULATORY REQUIREMENTS

Commercial bank regulations

Regulations pertaining to the participation of national banks in the interest rate futures market are outlined in Banking Circular No. 79, dated November 2, 1976. It generally defines the permissible activities as those that reduce the risk of interest rate fluctuations in the corresponding cash markets. A proposal for conducting such activities must be submitted to the Legal Advisory Services Division of the Comptroller of the Currency.

The application must include the following information:

1. The type of personnel that will assume responsibility for developing and administrating applications.
2. The trading limits that will be imposed.
3. Conditions that will permit deviations from these limits.
4. Procedures and controls that will prevent unauthorized trading.
5. Samples of forms that will be used to inform management daily of outstanding futures contract commitments.
6. Copies of internal record keeping forms in blank, which reflect the bank's daily futures contract activity with regard to maturities, current mark to market positions, gross and net futures positions, dollars held in margin accounts, profit or loss positions, and others.

Generally every interest rate futures transaction must correspond to an immediate or anticipated cash market transaction and be undertaken to substantially reduce the risk or loss exposure from such transactions.

If a cash transaction associated with a futures trade is not conducted simultaneously, an existing cash position may be used to meet this requirement. The following applications are candidates for the use of interest rate futures:

160

1. Improve management of anticipated cash flow by making purchases or sales in lieu of less advantageous cash markets.
2. Arbitrage existing fixed income portfolios.
3. Replace expiring maturities.
4. Hedge a certificate of deposit insurance program.
5. Firm up income from fixed-rate loans during times of rising interest rates.

For a more timely interpretation, it is suggested that the Comptroller's office be contacted directly.

Federal Home Loan Bank Board regulations

The Federal Home Loan Bank Board (FHLBB) amended Part 545 of the Rules and Regulations for the Federal Savings and Loan Systems by amending paragraph 545.9 by resolution no. 75-865 on September 30, 1975. Effective June 22, 1976, Part 545 was amended by adding a new paragraph 545.29. The pertinent points of this regulation are reviewed under the following classifications.

Eligibility requirements. Associations engaged in mortgage futures transactions must meet the net worth requirements of paragraph 563.13(b). Scheduled items cannot exceed 2.5 percent of specified assets, and all of appraised losses must be offset by a specified loss reserve.

Investment limitations. The total amount of gross mortgage futures position (the arithmetic sum of shorts and longs) may not exceed the net worth. Mortgage futures transactions must be associated with actual commitments or anticipated reinvestments in mortgages or mortgage-related securities over the forthcoming 12 months.

Record keeping. A register of all outstanding futures transactions must be maintained. This must be in a format that can be reviewed by senior management. In addition, records identifying specific futures transactions with a cash or anticipating cash transaction must be available.

A list of all authorized personnel who may trade and a statement of trading limits must be maintained. These documents must also provide for audit controls.

Notification. Each association engaged in mortgage futures trading must notify the District Director of Examinations at the Federal Home Loan Bank of which it is a member. Thereafter, it must notify the director quarterly of its outstanding positions.

These rules are designed to prevent misuse of the contracts and to insure the FHLBB that senior management is aware of all futures trading conducted by its staff. The rules enable an institution to participate in this market with minimal limitations.

ARBITRAGE OPPORTUNITIES

Many institutions have developed a securities trading profit center. This unit may be a department called Bank Investments, or perhaps only a senior officer who is skilled in the techniques of arbitrage. The activities may be limited to trading money market instruments or may include riding the yield curve (see page 170). Whether the trader has a position limit of $1 million or $100 million, the use of interest rate futures should become an accepted trading strategy.

If a sector swap looks advantageous between a corporate bond and a long-term Treasury bond, a trader should examine the feasibility of swapping the corporate bond against a long-term government interest rate contract.[1] If a GNMA looks cheap compared with a long-term government bond, could it be purchased for less in the futures market? If a yield curve is expected to flatten, can a cash position be protected by means of executing a futures contract? Can an accounting loss be accelerated or deferred?

These are the types of questions that should be asked by those responsible for generating trading profits and managing assets. The

---

[1] This is a swap between two bonds with dissimilar characteristics, i.e., safety, maturity.

following examples illustrate potential arbitrage applications for interest rate futures; they are by no means inclusive.

Fixed income arbitrage

There are several significant reasons for swapping bonds: first, to increase current earnings; second, to improve capital appreciation income by purchasing deep discount bonds; and third, to capital-ize on unusually attractive spread relationships between two bonds of similar quality and maturity. The latter reason is most suitable for the use of interest rate futures, since in some instances the bonds traded may never have to be owned by the investor. An example of such a substitution exchange is the swapping of a GNMA 8 for a GNMA 8.5.

GNMA 8's versus GNMA 8.5's. Table 10-1 has the necessary in-formation for a trader to determine the feasibility of positioning an arbitrage trade between these coupons.

From examination of this six-month data, several trading strate-gies can be formulated.[2] If the coupons are swapped in the cash market, it is assumed that a trader already owns GNMA 8's. The results generated by using the cash and futures markets inter-changeably are also compared.

It is apparent that on January 20, 1978, the price spread between coupons is unusually narrow. The trader sells GNMA 8's and buys GNMA 8.5's in the immediate cash market. The transaction is offset on April 28, 1978, with a net profit of 12/32.

	GNMA 8	GNMA 8.5
January 20	S 95-08	B 98-28
April 28	B 94-04	S 98-04
	+36	−24

If the transaction is accomplished by substituting futures for the GNMA 8 using the June futures contract, the net profit is 1/32.

---

[2] These basic analyses do not include the concept of reinvesting interest income or the cost of carrying charges.

	Sell			*Buy*			
	GNMA 8.000 07/01/05		versus	GNMA 8.500 07/01/05			
	Price			*Yield*			
Date	*8's* *sell* *bid*	*8.5's* *buy* *ask*	*8's* *sell* *bid*	*8.5's* *buy* *ask*		*Price* *spread*	*Yield* *spread*
01/20/78	95.250	98.875	8.779	8.764		−3.625	0.014
01/27/78	95.250	98.875	8.779	8.764		−3.625	0.014
02/03/78	95.156	98.875	8.793	8.764		−3.719	0.028
02/10/78	95.125	99.000	8.797	8.746		−3.875	0.051
02/24/78	94.875	98.875	8.835	8.764		−4.000	0.071
03/10/78	95.500	99.500	8.741	8.674		−4.000	0.067
03/17/78	95.625	99.750	8.722	8.637		−4.125	0.085
03/24/78	95.125	99.250	8.797	8.710		−4.125	0.088
03/31/78	94.625	98.625	8.873	8.801		−4.000	0.072
04/07/78	94.625	98.750	8.873	8.783		−4.125	0.090
04/14/78	94.750	99.000	8.854	8.746		−4.250	0.108
04/21/78	94.250	98.625	8.930	8.801		−4.375	0.129
04/28/78	94.000	98.250	8.968	8.856		−4.250	0.112
05/05/78	93.875	98.000	8.988	8.893		−4.125	0.095
05/12/78	93.375	97.625	9.065	8.949		−4.250	0.116
05/19/78	93.188	97.125	9.094	9.023		−3.938	0.071
05/26/78	92.625	96.125	9.181	9.174		−3.500	0.008
06/02/78	92.688	96.375	9.172	9.136		−3.688	0.036
Mean..						−3.977	0.070
Standard deviation of spread						0.248	0.036

Source: Docuswap, A Service of Cunningham & Company, Detroit, Michigan.

	GNMA June *1978 contract*	*Cash* *GNMA 8.5*
January 20	S 94-05	B 98-28
April 28	B 93-12	S 98-04
	+25	−24

In this instance, the cash versus cash trade is superior. The longer
the arbitrage position remains open, the less advantageous is a
short futures position, since convergence normally works against
the trader. Inversely, a long futures position is improved by time
when the yield curve is normal. To illustrate this, assume the same
arbitrage transaction is offset on February 24, 1978. The net
profit is 4/32.

	GNMA 8	GNMA 8.5
January 20	S 95-08	B 98-28
February 24	B 95-00	S 98-24
	+08	−04

If June 1978 futures are used instead of GNMA 8's, a net profit of 9/32 is obtained.

	GNMA June 1978 contract	Cash GNMA 8.5
January 20	S 94-05	B 98-28
February 24	B 93-24	S 98-24
	+13	−04

When the time frame is shortened, the result from a short futures trade against cash is generally superior.

In summary, when arbitrage opportunities are recognized, make the following observations before positioning your trade:

1. If a futures contract exists with a strong price correlation to the selected security, test its price level. If the price level of the contract supports a sell strategy, make certain that the time frame required for the arbitrage trade is short. This is less important when the yield curve is inverted.
2. Consider trading in the GNMA cash forward market versus GNMA or long-term government futures. This trade requires little cash and can offer significant opportunity.
3. Chart the spread and basis relationships between cash and futures.

ARBITRAGING A GOVERNMENT AUCTION

On November 3, 1978, the long-term U.S. government bond futures contract is trading at 92-02 at 10:00 A.M. Rumors are rampant that the new 30-year government bond to be auctioned that day will come to the market at a yield of 8.90 percent. Brokers assume that the new security will have either an 8¾ percent or 8⅝ percent coupon. The conversion factor for an 8¾ percent 30-year bond is 1.0848 and the factor for the 8⅝ percent is 1.0707.

An investor should now examine the yield levels at which an immediate profit can be assured through purchasing the bonds at an auction and redelivering them in the futures market.

Step 1: Look up the conversion factors in Treasury Bond Conversion Factors Manual No. 765 (Boston: Financial Publishing Co.) for 8⅝ percent and 8¾ percent coupons with a 30-year remaining maturity.

Coupon	Factor
8⅝	1.0707
8¾	1.0848

Step 2: Multiply the immediate long-term U.S. bond interest rate futures price by the above factor (92-02 = 92.0625).

$$92.0625 \times 1.0707 = 98.57$$
$$92.0625 \times 1.0848 = 99.86$$

Step 3: Convert the decimal price to 32ds.

$$98.57 = 98^{18}/_{32}$$
$$98.86 = 99^{28}/_{32}$$

Step 4: Look up the yields to maturity for the coupons at the above prices.

Coupon	Term	Price	Yield
8⅝	30 years	98-18	8.76
8¾	30 years	99-28	8.76

Step 5: Compute the prices of 8¾ percent and 8⅝ percent coupons with 30-year maturities, if they are to yield 8.90 percent as rumored on the morning of November 3, 1978.

Coupon	Yield to maturity	Price
8⅝	8.90	97-04
8¾	8.90	98-15

Based on the above analysis, an investor will generate the following profit per million if the bonds can be purchased at an 8.90 percent yield level and sold into the futures market:

	Coupon	
	858	834
Acquisition price on November 3	97-04	98-15
Deliver into futures market on December 1	98-18	99-28
Gross profit per $1 million	1-14	1-13
	$14,375	$14,062

Step 6: To arrive at a net profit from this computation, the investor must reduce the gross profit by the negative carry that was in existence during November 1978. The repo rate for government bonds is 9.80 percent. Since bonds purchased in the auction have a settlement date of November 15, 1978, they require 15 days of carry until they will be redelivered into the long-term U.S. government bond contract on December 1, 1978. In addition, the gross profit is reduced by a commission of $600 per $1 million.

In conclusion, this strategy will be successful at any bid level above 8.78 percent. The risk associated with this strategy is minimal. If a short futures position is taken and the investor is not successful in obtaining bonds in the auction, he or she will be exposed to a sudden upward price movement on the futures market. This can be minimized by placing a stop loss order and entering a conservative bid into the auction.

PROTECTING THE STANDBY WRITER

In Chapter 9 a section was devoted to the method of recovering standby fees paid to writers by mortgage originators. A similar approach can be used by GNMA standby writers who issue standbys that later become exposed to deliveries.

Making forward mortgage loan commitments is one of the riskiest tasks that can be undertaken by a mortgage lending intermediary.[3] The volatility of mortgage rates in recent years has caused lenders to be less willing to make such commitments. If the use of interest rate futures can lessen this risk, their emergence should be welcome by both lenders and borrowers.

The theory of this application revolves about protecting the net price of an insured standby commitment. If its strike price is 94-00 and the buyer pays a one-point nonrecoverable fee, then the writer does not experience an opportunity loss until market prices for immediate GNMA securities drop below 93-00. To minimize such a loss, the writer must develop a business plan that utilizes the concept of shorting a suitable GNMA futures contract. The writer may choose to short the total exposure at once or to protect a portion at a time as predetermined yield levels are touched. The most difficult decisions pertain to offsetting these positions if GNMA yield levels correct themselves while a short position is open. Since market movements seldom occur in a straight line, the danger of whiplash is always present. The business plan of the standby writer must define how quickly an open short position should be covered if interest rates begin to improve.[4]

The decision should differ between writers that have accumulated a profit in their hedge positions and those that have an almost immediate loss. Each situation must be analyzed based on the current interest rate level of the market, economic projections, and the remaining duration of the outstanding standby. A typical one-year GNMA standby commitment is usually written at a net price of 2.5 to 3.5 points less than current market levels. Therefore, yield levels must deteriorate markedly before a writer executes a short hedge.

---

[3] See Brian Smith and Kenneth J. Thygerson, "Hedging Forward Loan Commitments," Working Paper No. 12, U.S. League of Savings and Loan Associations, February 28, 1977.

[4] See Chapter 12.

Recognizing these preconditions, a business plan should be prepared that attempts to minimize major opportunity losses to the writer. These losses generally occur when the bond market is in a prolonged, steep downtrend, as was experienced in 1978. The futures trading strategy should attempt to protect gains, even at the risk of several reentries. If a short hedge position results in an almost immediate loss to the writer, a one-point tolerance level should be reasonably accommodated before offsetting the position. Both concepts can be illustrated by reviewing past market conditions.

Standby writer's strategy

If the Stratton Mutual Savings Bank writes a GNMA one-year standby on April 12, 1976, when GNMAs are yielding 8.07 and the FHA contract rate is 8.5 percent, the standby probably carries a strike price of 97-04 for an 8 percent GNMA security with an additional one-point nonrefundable fee. The immediate GNMA price must then drop below 96-04 before the writer is exposed to an opportunity loss. In the spring of 1976, this occurs almost immediately. By May 25, 1976, the writer decides to seek hedge protection using the GNMA futures contract when the immediate GNMA price drops below 96-04. The September 1976 contract is selected for short hedging because the yield curve is flattening rapidly and Stratton wants to avoid being short in a back month. There is complete awareness that the September 1976 contract expires before the standby and may require rolling forward into another contract if the hedge remains open until the standby expires. Ten September 1976 contracts are shorted by Stratton at 97-14. Within two weeks, prices begin to improve, and this hedge position never accumulates a significant favorable balance. Simultaneously, long-term rates begin to stabilize and the net cash inflow into thrift institutions starts to improve. By June 13, the short position has lost one point, and the Stratton Mutual Savings Bank offsets its short position according to the business plan. The thrift institution has now dissipated the one-point fee received earlier for writing this standby.

On the other hand, if the bond market continues to lose ground after the hedge is placed on May 25, 1976, Stratton will continue to maintain its short position. If a sizable profit is earned from this position, it could be protected by a buy stop order that can be moved up or down daily, depending on market conditions. This strategy will preserve some of the accumulated gains if yields return to the level where the hedge was initiated.

In conclusion, this application does not lend itself easily to a predetermined formula. Trading strategies must be tailored to specific situations. Losses may occur. However, the prudent use of futures can minimize opportunity losses and thereby encourage greater standby writing activity.

YIELD CURVE TRADING

Bond investors and speculators can use the present and anticipated shape of a yield curve to develop investment and trading strategies. A thorough analysis of the curve enables them to project the profits of various patterns. Figure 10-1 is illustrative of the many shapes that have evolved in recent years.

Since most curves flatten with increasing maturities, the expression "riding a yield curve" depicts a rider mounting the curve on its gentler slope and sliding on its contour to the end of the line. The steeper the slope, the wider is the yield curve and the more rewarding it is for the classic investor who buys a security with a one- or two-year maturity and sells it when its maturity is reduced to 90-120 days.

In its most basic use, riding a yield curve can be illustrated by buying a 182-day Treasury bill in the regular weekly auction, holding the bill for 90-120 days, and then selling it at higher prices. The proceeds from the sale are reinvested in a new-issue 182-day Treasury bill. If this can be done persistently, an investor can measurably increase the effective yield of a 90-day T-bill investment.

Assume that I. M. Fast buys a 182-day Treasury bill yielding 7.00 percent discounted. If Fast holds it for 91 days and sells it in the

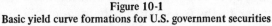

Figure 10-1
Basic yield curve formations for U.S. government securities

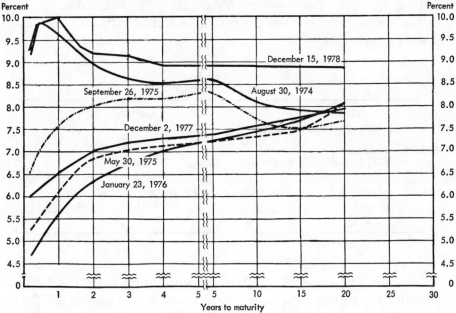

Source: Federal Reserve Bank of St. Louis.

cash market for 6.50 percent, a profit of 50 basis points is generated. When added to the 7.00 percent on a 91-day investment, an actual discount yield of 7.50 percent is earned.

This type of trading occasionally can be optimized by using the T-bill futures market. If I. M. Fast needs to purchase a 91-day T-bill on March 20, 1978, Fast could make the following observations.

Upon examining the yield curve, Fast finds a difference of 37 BP between a 91- and a 182-day T-bill. The actual discount yields are 6.23 and 6.60 respectively. Fast also examines the T-bill futures market and determines that the June contract is trading at an IMM index of 93.32, or a yield of 6.68. Fast decides it is now possible to buy the 182-day T-bill in the cash market, sell a June 1978 T-bill contract, and deliver September 21, 1978, bills whose remaining maturity is 91 days on June 22 against the short T-bill.

171

By transacting both legs of the trade simultaneously, Fast locks in a yield superior to the 6.23 percent that was attainable if a 91-day T-bill had been purchased on March 20, 1978 (see Table 10-2). This transaction improves the return on this investment by $732, less commissions.

Table 10-2
Comparative earnings

Cash only		Cash and futures	
Purchase and sell 91-day T-bill			
3/20 Purchase at 6.23 percent . . .	$ 984,252	3/20 Purchase 182-day T-bill at 6.60 percent	$966,634
6/22 Redemption	1,000,000	6/22 Sell through T-bill futures	983,114
Profit	$ 15,748	Profit	$ 16,480

An additional example of riding the yield curve using the T-bill contract is to buy or sell the nearby contract and buy or sell the fourth or fifth option. In effect, the trader is positioning a spread between the 91-day T-bill and the one year T-bill. This trade is based on the assumption that the second, third, and fourth options reflect the approximate yield levels of 180-, 270-, and 360-day T-bills. Although this is theoretical, it can be applied by a speculator with a great degree of success.

If I. M. Fast determines on December 30, 1976, that the one-year versus 3-month yield curves will widen appreciably during the next six months, he should buy the nearby contract and sell the fourth option. Figure 10-2 can be used to track this trade by analyzing the spread between the first and fourth T-bill options during the first six months of 1977.

Hedging a widening yield curve

On December 30, 1976, the one-year versus three-month yield differential is 38 basis points. This increases to 77 BP by March 18, 1977, and narrows to 56 BP by April 15, 1977.

172

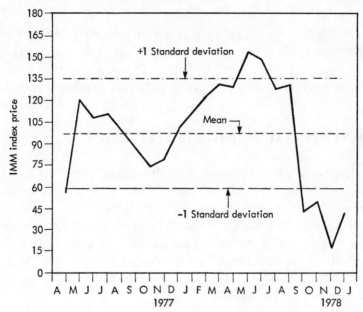

Figure 10-2
Price spread analysis of first versus fourth 90-day T-bill futures contracts

Source: Telerate Historical Data Base, Rapidata, Inc.

If Fast wants to trade his expectations that the curve will widen, the following spread could be established on January 3, 1977:

> Buy one March 1977 T-bill at 95.40
> Sell one December 1977 T-bill at 94.44

On March 18, these contracts could be offset at the following prices:

> Sell one March 1977 T-bill at 95.41
> Buy one December 1977 T-bill at 93.43

The gross profit from this spread transaction is $2,550 per contract. This profit is generated without investing any cash other than the required margin deposits. If I. M. Fast desires to maintain a spread position beyond March 22, this will necessitate closing out the March leg and rolling the long position forward into the June T-bill contract. If Fast believes that the yield curve will

173

flatten again, the long position could be transferred to a 1978 contract.

These T-bill futures applications are merely representative of the numerous trading opportunities that are sometimes available. They should be sufficient to stimulate one's curiosity to pursue independent study into other cross-hedging opportunities.

CONVENTIONAL MORTGAGE SECURITIES

Mortgage-related obligations are the largest and most rapidly growing sector of American debt.[5] In 1978 GNMA mortgage-backed securities became shelf items in the fixed income industry. Their success has been a catalyst in bringing similar nongovernment guaranteed mortgage securities into the marketplace. Lending institutions with real estate portfolios are eager for the opportunity to sell these assets selectively or to utilize them for collateral against additional debt.

In September 1977 the Bank of America issued the first major, private conventional mortgage-backed security for $150 million. The funds were used to increase the lending capability of the institution. In addition, the instrument generated a profit potential, since the loans sold or used for collateral were closed at a higher yield than the coupon of the mortgage security. Since 1977 the private sector has issued more than $2 billion of mortgage bonds and mortgage-backed securities.

The bonds are debt instruments, whereas the mortgage-backed securities represent a sale of assets. The bonds are generally over-collateralized to obtain a satisfactory credit rating; their terms may vary. The mortgage-backed securities are priced and sold at an average life of 12 years. The actual mortality experience associated with these pools must be individually calculated since every issuing lending institution has its own payoff, delinquency, and foreclosure characteristics.

---

[5] See Table 2-1.

The Federal Home Loan Mortgage Corporation (FHLMC), which was established in 1970, can also be considered a nongovernment issuer of mortgage-backed securities. It is a corporate instrumentality of the United States. The FHLMC was established to improve the secondary market for residential conventional loans. It performs this function by buying qualified loans primarily from regulated thrift institutions and some selected mortgage bankers through an auction similar to that for FNMAs. It can sell these loans in various forms, including a mortgage-backed security called a mortgage participation certificate (sometimes referred to as PCs). These securities are similar to GNMAs in all respects but guarantee and monthly payments method. Table 10-3 is a summary of certain pertinent information concerning the Federal Home Loan Mortgage Corporation's offerings of mortgage participation certificates, which have been available continually since 1972.

Figure 10-3
Summary: Mortgage participation certificates

The following is a summary of certain pertinent information concerning the Federal Home Loan Mortgage Corporation's offerings of mortgage participation certificates.

PCs offered

The PCs . . . . The PCs represent undivided interests in specified first lien residential conventional mortgages in groups aggregating approximately $100 to $200 million underwritten and owned by the mortgage corporation. Fees are paid to purchasers under certain programs as described below.

Interest . . . . Passed through monthly at the certificate rate.

Principal . . . . Passed through monthly, as collected.

Prepayment fees . . . . Passed through when and if received as additional income over and above interest at the certificate rate.

Guarantees . . . . The mortgage corporation unconditionally guarantees the timely payment of interest at the certificate rate and collection of principal as described below.

Remittances . . . . . . One itemized check per month containing principal, interest, and prepayment fees is normally mailed five calendar days prior to the fifteenth day of each month. A purchaser of a PC will receive the first remittance on or before the fifteenth day of the

Figure 10-3 *(continued)*

Remittances *(continued)*	second month following the month in which the purchaser becomes a registered holder of the PC on the books and records of the mortgage corporation.
Denominations and registration	$100,000, $200,000, $500,000 and $1,000,000; fully registered only.
Federal tax status ...	PCs owned by institutions that qualify as "domestic building and loan associations" constitute "loans secured by an interest in real property" within the meaning of Section 7701(a)(19)(C)(v) of the Internal Revenue Code; PCs also constitute "qualifying real property loans" within the meaning of Section 593(d) of the code with respect to certain thrift institutions.
FHLBB regulatory matters	For institutions the deposits or accounts of which are insured by the Federal Savings and Loan Insurance Corporation, PCs are to be reported to the Federal Home Loan Bank Board in the asset classification "Mortgages, participations, or mortgage-backed securities insured or guaranteed by an agency or instrumentality of the U.S.," and PCs current with respect to guaranteed principal and interest payments are not "scheduled items," notwithstanding the performance of any underlying loan; for federally chartered savings and loan associations, PCs are exempt from all percent of assets lending limitations.
Secondary market ...	Certain securities dealers and the mortgage corporation make a market in PCs.

The mortgage corporation guarantees to each registered holder of a PC the timely payment of interest accruing at the applicable certificate rate on the unpaid principal balance outstanding on the mortgages to the extent of such holder's percentage of participation therein. The mortgage corporation also guarantees to each registered holder of a PC collection of all principal on the mortgages, without any offset or deduction, to the extent of such holder's percentage of participation therein. The PCs are not guaranteed by the United States or by any of the Federal Home Loan Banks and do not constitute a debt or obligation of the United States or any Federal Home Loan Bank.

Source: Federal Home Loan Mortgage Corporation.

Table 10-3 identifies the institutional population that owns PCs as of January 1, 1978.

Since conventional mortgages represent more than 80 percent of the U.S. residential mortgage debt, the growth of conventional securities is only a matter of time and appropriate interest rate

Table 10-3
Ownership of participation certificates, January 1, 1978

Holder	Number of holders	Percent of all holders	Unpaid principal balance held ($ millions)	Percent of total unpaid principal balance
Savings and loans	1,194	66.0%	$2,545.1	47.63%
Credit unions	181	10.0	179.7	3.37
Commercial banks	86	4.7	85.7	1.60
Savings banks	44	2.4	50.9	0.94
Private pension plans	26	1.4	30.6	0.57
Public pension plans	27	1.5	205.1	3.84
Insurance companies	22	1.2	33.3	0.62
Individuals	19	1.0	1.9	0.04
Corporations/partnerships . . .	15	0.8	36.2	0.68
Brokers, dealers, agents	24	1.3	640.9	12.00
Nominees	155	8.5	1,484.4	27.79
Others	20	1.2	49.2	0.92
Total	1,813	100.0%	$5,343.0	100.00%

Source: Federal Home Loan Bank Board.

levels. It has been estimated by the American Bankers Association that more than $100 billion of this type of security could be issued by 1988. If this forecast is correct, it must be possible to protect the value of these securities and their origination in a manner similar to the protection of insured loans and GNMAs.

Currently the price movement of PCs lags the GNMA market. They are traded with larger spreads since their secondary market is not yet fully developed. Based on their 1978 price movements, their correlations can be considered sufficiently positive to permit cross hedging. The philosophy of hedging a conventional portfolio is appropriate. Since the correlation coefficient between a PC, a conventional mortgage-backed security, and a GNMA is acceptable over extended periods, the use of the GNMA interest rate futures contract is considered potentially valid when properly designed.[6] When and if a futures contract is developed based on a conventional mortgage, this process will be far more reliable.

The following simulated cross-hedge transaction depicts a typical result.

Optimizing anticipated cash flow

On June 1, 1976, the investment officer of the pension fund of the Ice-O-Matic Corporation becomes aware that $5 million of corporate securities will be redeemed in December 1976. After carefully analyzing available economic data, the investment officer is convinced that interest rates will be lower in December 1976. In addition, the pension manager asks the officer to consider purchasing PCs, since their yield levels appear abnormally high when compared to those of other corporates.

The following hedge strategy is devised:

	Cash market	Futures market
June 1, 1976	Defer any action until December	Buy 50 GNMA December 1976 contracts at 93-18
December 1, 1976	Use funds from redemption to buy $5 million in PCs in immediate market	Sell 50 GNMA December 1976 contracts at 100-17

The futures transaction results in a $348,437 profit. This is applied to increase the yield level of the $5 million of 7.5 percent PCs, which were purchased on December 1, 1976, yielding 7.641 percent at a price of 98.0625. If these bonds had been purchased on June 1, 1976, they would have been acquired at a yield of 8.669 percent, or a price of 90.625. The difference is an opportunity loss of $74,375 per $1 million. On a $5 million transaction, the opportunity loss would be $371,875. When this is compared with the gross profit of $348,437, it becomes obvious that the anticipatory cross hedge is satisfactory.

---

[6] See Lillian D. Ratner, "Another Look at GNMA Futures Market Hedging," *Savings Bank Journal,* April 1977.

Chapter
11

Home builder applications

HEDGING SINGLE-FAMILY PERMANENT LOAN COMMITMENTS

A profitable home sales program requires a good location, a desirable product that is competitively priced, and the availability of permanent financing. To assure potential buyers of reasonably priced mortgage funds, a builder must purchase a permanent commitment from a thrift institution at the time construction commences.[1] Often this is also a prerequisite to obtaining a construction loan commitment.

Most permanent commitments are negotiated for a dollar amount within a specific time period. The mortgage rate also may be negotiated when the commitment is purchased or, simply stated, at the market rate upon closing. The latter would probably be more desirable for the lending institution but riskier for the builder,

---

[1] This commitment is for long-term mortgage loans as opposed to short-term construction loans.

179

since buyers are rate conscious and often select a house based on the amount of their monthly payments. A 0.5 percent increase in a mortgage rate associated with a 30-year term increases monthly payments by $0.36 per $1,000. Thus, a noncompetitive mortgage rate can quickly disqualify a potential buyer. To minimize underwriting problems, builders prefer to pay a larger nonrecoverable commitment fee in return for obtaining a guaranteed funding rate when the commitment is negotiated.

With the advent of the GNMA mortgage interest rate futures contract, a builder should examine the alternative of using this contract in conjunction with a market rate permanent loan commitment.[2] This combination may provide the necessary insurance that a takeout will be available at competitive rates. This is especially true during periods of improving or stable interest rates.

To determine the feasibility of this approach, two case studies have been developed. The first reviews a financing technique in conjunction with a conventional loan program, and the second study examines the results of a hedge in conjunction with obtaining insured end loans.

"Case study assumptions"

It has been determined that a conventional market rate takeout for one year costs the Horizon Building Corporation a 0.5-point nonrefundable fee. If a maximum mortgage rate is negotiated at commitment time, it costs Horizon one point for a takeout commitment that has a 0.75 percent ceiling above the current conventional mortgage rate for 80 percent loan to value applications.[3] The immediate difference to Horizon is a savings of $5,000 per $1 million of permanent funds reserved if a market rate commitment is selected instead of a fixed-rate takeout.

---

[2] Permanent mortgages are closed at the rate in existence at the time a buyer is qualified and approved.

[3] See Kenneth J. Thygerson and Dennis J. Jacobe, "Mortgage Portfolio Management" (United States League of Savings Associations, 1978), p. 52.

Developing a business plan for obtaining conventional permanent loan commitments

A financing technique using the GNMA futures contract as a cross hedge can be executed by Horizon in the following manner:

1. Horizon negotiates a permanent takeout commitment for $1 million of conventional loans, to be closed within one year at market rates. This costs a nonrefundable fee of 0.5 point. This commitment must be compared with the alternative, which would provide Horizon with a $1 million takeout for one year at a maximum mortgage rate of 0.75 percent above the current rate for an 80 percent loan to value mortgage application. This would cost one point, nonrefundable. On July 1, 1977, the current rate is 8.75 percent. Therefore, such a commitment carries a maximum takeout rate of 9.5 percent for 80 percent loan to value applications.
2. By accepting a market rate commitment Horizon will be at a competitive disadvantage only if the permanent mortgage rate for the project exceeds 9.5 percent at the time of closings. Until then, or just prior to that time, no further action is required by the Horizon management. If mortgage rates remain stable or improve during the construction and sales cycle, no additional financing expense will ever be incurred.
3. Horizon's management decides that it must always be prepared to be competitive. They wish to assure buyers of a mortgage rate ceiling of 9.5 percent if rates escalate rapidly. Horizon develops a business plan with the following triggers:
   a. If the FNMA conventional four-month auction rate exceeds 9.40 percent, they will hedge half their mortgage requirements by shorting GNMA mortgage interest rate futures contracts.[4]
   b. If the FNMA conventional weighted average yield exceeds 9.50 percent, they will short an additional quantity of GNMA futures contracts equal to their remaining need.
   c. These positions will be offset when a sale occurs and the buyer obtains permanent financing, or when mortgage

---

[4] The FNMA results are quoted semimonthly in *The Wall Street Journal.*

interest rates improve to a level less than 9.40 percent, as reflected by the FNMA conventional auction.

d. Any profits earned from these transactions will be used to obtain a below-market-rate closing from the thrift institution that sold Horizon the permanent commitment.

Before reviewing the results of the Horizon strategy, it must be understood that the correlation between the GNMA futures contract and conventional loans is not always satisfactory when measured by a correlation coefficient.[5] However, a partial recovery may still be a superior solution for Horizon when the other associated advantages of this strategy are considered.

Analysis of results from Horizon's acceptance of a one-year commitment at market rate for $1 million of permanent conventional loans on July 1, 1977

Step 1: On July 1, 1977, a one-year loan commitment at the conventional market rate is closed, with a provision for rate suppression based on 1.75 points per 0.25 percent mortgage rate. A $5,000 nonrefundable fee is paid to the thrift institution.

Step 2: No further action is required until February 6, 1978, when the FNMA weighted average for conventional loans exceeds 9.40 percent at the biweekly auction. Horizon is now required to short five GNMA contracts according to its business plan. A $5,000 initial margin deposit is made with a broker and an IVT is performed. On February 7, 1978, Horizon instructs its broker to sell five September 1978 contracts at 93-25.

Step 3: Interest rates continue to increase quickly, and at the next FNMA auction the average weighted rate for conventional loans exceeds 9.50 percent. Horizon shorts five more September 1978 contracts at a price of 93-01 on February 21, 1978. Another $5,000 initial margin is required.

---

[5] See Brian Smith and Kenneth J. Thygerson, "Hedging Forward Loan Commitments," Working Paper No. 12, U.S. League of Savings and Loan Associations, February 28, 1977.

Step 4: During the first three weeks of March, the GNMA market noticeably improves, although the FNMA conventional auction fails to reflect this movement. Horizon is exposed to a margin call of $7,500 four weeks after shorting the second five contracts, but it does not offset the position since the conventional FNMA weighted average holds firm.

Step 5: The GNMA market resumes its downward trend on March 23, 1978, and by March 29, the September contract is again trading at 93-01. Horizon is now beginning to build up a debit balance.

Step 6: The futures positions remain open until closings take place. Six units close in April 1978 and the thrift institution makes 9.5 percent mortgages. This necessitates no further action on the part of Horizon management. Since the average mortgage balance per unit is $65,000, Horizon offsets four futures contracts. On April 13, 1978, they buy back four September 1978 contracts at 92-25. This generates a profit of $1,000, which is placed into a reserve account that can be used to suppress mortgage rates for future buyers. The initial margin associated with these contracts is also returned.

Step 7: On June 9, 1978, the remaining units are delivered. The thrift institution qualifies the buyers at 9.75 percent, which is the current market rate. Upon request, the thrift institution is willing to suppress the mortgage rate 0.25 percent for 1.75 points, or $1,750 per $100,000. Horizon offsets the remaining six September 1978 contracts at a price of 90-27. The profit generated from this transaction is $16,892.50. The remaining initial margin deposits associated with this transaction are also returned. The trading profits are retained by Horizon since their buyers can qualify at 9.75 percent and no demand is made to lower the rate.

In summary, this strategy accomplishes the following results:

1. It assures Horizon of obtaining end loans for its buyers.
2. It enables Horizon to minimize the finance expenses associated with obtaining permanent commitments.
3. It gives Horizon management maximum flexibility in directing

its end loan business at the time of closing. It will lose only 0.5 point if the buyers are directed to an alternate lender.

4. It enables Horizon to earn an additional $17,892.50, less commission, per $1 million, since the funds are not required to suppress mortgage commitment rates to buyers. If necessary, $17,500 should suppress a mortgage rate by 0.25 percent for $1 million of conventional residential loans.

The risks associated with this strategy are related primarily to the correlation of the price movement of the GNMA mortgage interest rate contract and conventional loans. As can be observed from this example, during the first three weeks in March, Horizon experienced a negative correlation. Conventional rates increased, while insured rates as measured by the GNMA market improved. It can also be noted from weekly FHLMC reports that conventional rates vary greatly between geographic areas at any one time, making it more difficult to establish a precise correlation to a project.

Therefore, home builders who use this approach must be aware of its risks as well as its rewards. This hedging strategy should be planned with the advice of a knowledgeable interest rate futures analyst.

HEDGING AN INSURED SINGLE-FAMILY BUILDER COMMITMENT

If on July 1, 1977, Horizon applies for an insured $1 million, one-year, single-family commitment, its rate will be tied to a GNMA security yield level. On June 27, 1977, GNMA 8's in the immediate market are priced at par. Therefore, a one-year commitment is available at 97-16, with an additional one point up front. If Horizon's management declines this offer, they can pursue their own hedge program, which incorporates the following strategy:

1. When the GNMA immediate market price exceeds a GNMA yield of 8.30 percent, which represents the equivalent yield level available to Horizon on July 1, 1977, the builder will hedge 100 percent of the requirements in the futures market.
2. A short futures position will be offset in the following manner:

a. When a sale occurs and a buyer is qualified, an equal dollar value of futures is offset.

b. If interest rates improve and the open contracts have a mark to market loss of 24/32, 50 percent of the remaining contracts will be offset. The last contract will be offset when the mark to market loss reaches 40/32.

This strategy limits the loss of Horizon to a maximum of one point if it is not required to reenter the futures market at a later date. This point is equal to the nonrefundable fee that would be charged by the mortgage company for a commitment fee.

3. Horizon plans to sell all its loans in the immediate cash market, since this is generally the most competitive strategy for its purposes.

4. Horizon will build four points into the cost of its units for financing purposes. Two points must be available up front, since they may be required for hedging on a commodity exchange.

Since the correlation between the GNMA mortgage interest rate futures contract and insured mortgage rates is high, the results of this strategy can be expected to be very satisfactory.[6]

Analysis of results derived from Horizon's decision to hedge the permanent insured end loan requirements with interest rate futures, instead of purchasing a one-year fixed rate commitment from the Unbelievable Mortgage Company

Step 1:   On July 1, 1977 a decision is made to self-insure Horizon's insured end loan requirements through hedging on a commodity exchange. Since the July 1 immediate bid price for GNMA 8's is 100-00, no further action is required to keep Horizon competitive.

Step 2:   From July through September, the debt market is stable. It begins to deteriorate in October and triggers 97-16 during the first week of November 1977. On November 8, 1977, Horizon sells ten September 1978

---

[6] Correlation is 96 percent, according to 1975 CBOT studies.

contracts at 96-09. The delay in entering the market promptly is a management decision. An initial margin deposit of $10,000 is required.

Step 3: On March 17, 1978, Horizon delivers its first ten units. It sells $400,000 of loans to a mortgage company at 4.5 points for immediate delivery. This generates a loss of $2,000, since only 4 points are built into the units for financing costs. (The change in the FHA contract rate has no effect on this transaction.) Horizon now closes four contracts by buying them back at 93-31. This generates a profit of $9,250. This money is put into a reserve account that is available to subsidize any necessary financing costs above 4 points.

Step 4: On June 19, the remaining units are sold and the mortgages are placed with a mortgage company at 6.5 points. This is 2.5 points, or $15,000, more, based on the remaining mortgage balance of $600,000, than was originally built into the units for financing. Horizon then closes out its last six September 1978 contracts at a price of 90-27. This generates an additional profit of $30,750, which is sufficient to offset the $15,000 financing loss.

The total profit from this strategy is $23,000 less commissions.

In summary, this concept merits the attention of single-family builders who understand the risks and the concepts of interest rate futures trading. The largest loss exposure from this strategy would occur if interest rate levels significantly improved during the fall of 1977 and then reversed themselves once more during the first half of 1978. This might have caused Horizon to buy back its position in 1977 at a loss and later come back into a short position for a second time. Whether or not a builder can assume such risks must determine the selection of this alternative.

HEDGING A SINGLE-FAMILY CONSTRUCTION LOAN

Many single-family construction loans are tied to a New York bank prime rate. On a few occasions a builder may negotiate for a fixed-rate construction loan. Since a fixed-rate construction loan carries

186

an initial lending rate greater than that of an equivalent loan tied to prime, the motivation to obtain such a lending agreement must be a fear of inflation. If a borrower is confident that the total interest expense associated with a subdivision can be controlled through the prudent use of interest rate futures, it is likely that few builders will select a fixed-rate construction loan.

The 90-day T-bill contract is the most likely candidate to accomplish this objective. The T-bill contract is effective in cross hedging interest rate risks associated with other short-term money market instruments. For example, the correlation coefficient between three-month certificates of deposit and 13-week T-bills is .854.[7] A similar study of T-bills versus prime commercial paper resulted in a correlation coefficient of .855.[8] Figure 11-1 depicts the yield movements of T-bills, the prime rate, and federal funds. It can be assumed that the correlation coefficient between T-bills and the

Figure 11-1
Yield relationship among T-bills, prime rate,
and federal funds

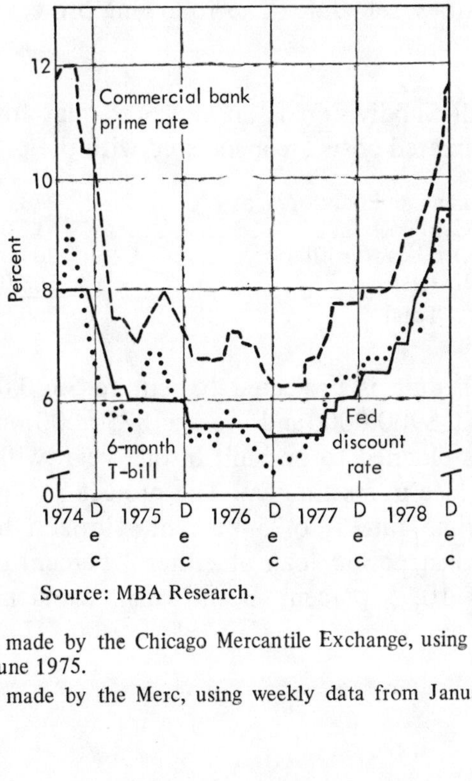

Source: MBA Research.

---

[7] From studies made by the Chicago Mercantile Exchange, using weekly data from January 1973 to June 1975.

[8] From studies made by the Merc, using weekly data from January 1973 to June 1975.

prime rate is slightly less than that between T-bills and other money market instruments since the prime rate is frequently controlled and moves in incremental steps.

If a builder selects a construction loan tied to the prime rate and desires to hedge the additional expense exposure associated with rising prime rates, the T-bill contract can be used until the commercial paper contract improves its liquidity.

The hedging strategy used is different from one developed to hedge the value of an asset. In this application the builder is interested in recovering the additional expense derived from a rise in the prime rates. This is a function of the prime rate and the amount of money outstanding at any time during construction. If the prime rate increases from the time of the second inspection to closing, it will be more expensive than if it had peaked at the first draw and receded thereafter.

In order to use an interest rate futures contract to hedge a variable-rate construction loan, the Horizon Building Corporation must simulate its draw schedule. The following project can be used as an example.

The Whitehall Subdivision is an approved plat for 20 units. The following estimated costs are associated with the project:

Land and development .... $	276,000
Hard costs	612,000
Overhead/profit	204,000
Interest	108,000
Total	$1,200,000

The draw schedule is projected to require $300,000 at the first draw, peak at $900,000, and average $750,000 outstanding. The subdivision is planned to be built in one year, with the first closings taking place in six months. The project begins in May 1977, when the prime rate is 6.75 percent. Horizon has a choice of selecting a construction loan at either 3 percent over prime or a fixed rate of 10.75 percent. Both loans have identical terms and conditions.

Management calculates that a fixed-rate loan will generate an interest expense of $80,625. If they accept the variable-rate loan, the following expenses are projected:

If rates remain constant
throughout the year $73,125

If prime is lowered to average
5.75 percent throughout
this building cycle $65,625

If prime averages 9.0 percent
during this building cycle $90,000

Therefore, the risk-reward ratio of this project based on available economic forecasts is a possible loss of $9,375 versus a potential gain of $15,000, if a variable rate structure is selected. This equates itself to a 1.6 to 1 risk reward ratio. This is a go signal for the variable-rate construction loan. This ratio can be improved by the use of interest rate futures, which make the variable-rate loan even more attractive to Horizon.

Horizon develops a business plan based on the following assumptions:

1. Initial draw is $300,000.
2. First draw per unit is 35 percent of hard cost.
3. Second draw per unit is 66 percent of hard cost.
4. No more than six unsold units under construction.
5. Average amount of loan outstanding is $750,000.

It is decided that no hedge action will be taken until the prime rate touches 7.75 percent. At that time a hedging strategy using the T-bill contract will be executed in the following manner:

1. An estimate of additional exposure should be made. This is greatly dependent on the time during the construction cycle when the prime rate hits 7.75 percent. If this occurs during the first three months of the project, the additional exposure in terms of dollars can be significant. If prime reaches 7.75 percent after half the units are closed, the exposure will be less.
2. After the dollar amount of exposure is estimated, it must be converted into a T-bill price move that will offset this loss. For

instance, if the additional exposure from increasing the prime rate is estimated as $5,000 for a specific construction loan, the hedger must understand that its recovery will necessitate a 2 percent yield change in one 90-day T-bill contract. Since such a high-velocity move is not probable in a short period of time, a cross hedge requires several T-bill contracts. The actual number of contracts shorted and the contract month selected must be decided upon when the hedge is placed.

On October 24, 1977, the prime rate increases to 7.75 percent. Horizon estimates its remaining additional expense due to continually increasing prime rates at $3,000 for the remainder of the project. They decide to hedge three T-bill contracts, since it is reasonable to assume, based on economic forecasts, that 90-day T-bill interest rates will increase by 40 basis points during the remaining construction period.

On October 25, 1977, Horizon places an order to short three June 1978 T-bill contracts. They are executed at 93.10. The construction loan is paid off on June 1, 1978. The prime rate has risen to 8.75 percent and the T-bill contract is offset at 92.90. Although successful, this hedge only partially recovers the increased cost incurred. Since the prime has remained less than 7.75 percent for the first half of the construction cycle, the average prime rate for the project is 8 percent. The total interest expense is computed at $82,500, or $1,875, above the interest expense associated with the fixed-rate option.

Although the illustrated T-bill hedge is imperfect in recapturing this amount, it succeeds in earning $1,500 without being exposed to any significant margin calls. By applying more sophisticated hedging techniques, the results of the T-bill hedge could be improved during this period. However, the T-bill rate was low on June 1, 1978, when compared with federal funds trading at 8 percent during this time.

In conclusion, this technique should be understood by all builders. Its application is suitable when the following conditions prevail:

1. Risk-reward ratio is greater than 1:5. However, this is a business decision.

2. The longer the time cycle of the project, the greater is the potential of this strategy.
3. When other short-term interest rate futures contracts develop sufficient liquidity, they too should be considered as hedging vehicles.

It is obvious that interest rate futures have a place in a home builder's tool kit. They cannot eliminate higher interest rates, difficulty in qualifying buyers, or the problem of finding permanent financing. They can be used effectively to reduce the costs associated with obtaining permanent financing and to control the expenses related to construction lending.

Chapter 12

Pitfalls of commodity trading

Trading a commodity contract can be compared to riding in a steeplechase. The obstacles are numerous and frequently unforeseen. The winning rider is not always the best equestrian but is frequently the most prudent tactician. Likewise, a good commodity trader is not always the most knowledgeable economist. A trader must be aware of current events and critical dates associated with the release of public data that may affect interest rates and their basic values. As an example, the announcement on July 6, 1978, of an economic summit meeting to be held on July 16, 1978, by the seven major non-Communist industrial nations had a significant impact on interest rate futures. The balance of trade problems in existence during 1978 were on the agenda. If progress ultimately is made toward easing the U.S. deficit and thereby improving the value of the American dollar, long-term interest rates should be favorably affected. If a workable agreement cannot be negotiated, then the present inflation rate may continue or even accelerate. Assessing these variables is a challenge for the trader. Whether to offset a position or take a new position on July 6, 1978, in anticipation of this meeting was an important decision. Similarly, both hedgers and traders must be aware that every Thursday afternoon the Federal Reserve System releases its "money numbers" (M1 and M2) for the prior week. Experts have found them difficult to estimate with any degree of consistent accuracy. Since both of these statistics have an immediate influence on interest rates, taking a position on a Thursday morning may be more risky or immediately rewarding for a speculator than buying or selling a contract on a Monday afternoon.

To enhance your ability to trade successfully, the following pitfalls should be recognized, since they repeatedly affect the results of interest rate futures transactions.

TAILORING STOP LOSS ORDERS

All too often hedgers and speculators place a stop loss order, or a limit order, and then promptly ignore their position. This is fundamentally incorrect. If a stop loss or limit price is selected on a technical basis, it might be excusable not to review the position in a timely manner. However, if the price level is selected to arbitrarily limit a loss or protect a profit, the trader must realize that in an active bull or bear market, daily price movements are more pronounced. Thus, placing a stop loss order 16/32 below a current price may be a prudent decision in an orderly market but improper during an active one. Similarly, if a trader wishes to protect a gain, stop loss orders must be moved up continuously. Their placement is related to two factors. The primary one is the trader's desire or need to protect an established gain or minimize a potential loss. The second factor is the trading history of a security.

If it can be determined that a 16/32 daily price movement is normal for a contract, then placing a stop loss order 16/32 below the current price is unwise. The trader unwittingly will be assured of being stopped out within a few days. To arrive at an appropriate stop loss position, review the available technical data pertaining to the contract and determine the amount of equity that can be lost in association with a trading position. Figure 12-1 is an excerpt from a study of GNMA price movements that were analyzed by the CBOT Research Department to arrive at the recommenda-

Figure 12-1
Simulated margin requirements study based on price movements
of GNMA 8's in cash market

			LONG				SHORT		
DATE	PRICE	: DR	CR	CALL	MARGIN A/C	: DR	CR	CALL	MARGIN A/C
10275	94.000	: ****	****	****	1500	: ****	****	****	1500
10375	94.750	: 0	750	0	2250	: 750	0	750	750
10675	94.000	: 750	0	0	1500	: 0	750	0	2250
10775	94.750	: 0	750	0	2250	: 750	0	0	1500
10875	94.750	: 0	0	0	2250	: 0	0	0	1500
10975	95.250	: 0	500	0	2750	: 500	0	500	1000
11075	95.500	: 0	250	0	3000	: 250	0	0	1250
11375	96.000	: 0	500	0	3500	: 500	0	750	750
11475	96.000	: 0	0	0	3500	: 0	0	0	1500
11575	96.000	: 0	0	0	3500	: 0	0	0	1500
11675	96.000	: 0	0	0	3500	: 0	0	0	1500
11775	96.000	: 0	0	0	3500	: 0	0	0	1500
12075	96.750	: 0	750	0	4250	: 750	0	750	750
12175	96.750	: 0	0	0	4250	: 0	0	0	1500
12275	96.500	: 250	0	0	4000	: 0	250	0	1750
12375	96.750	: 0	250	0	4250	: 250	0	0	1500
12475	96.750	: 0	0	0	4250	: 0	0	)	1500
12775	97.000	: 0	250	0	4500	: 250	0	)	1250
12875	97.000	: 0	0	0	4500	: 0	0	0	1250
12975	97.000	: 0	0	0	4500	: 0	0	0	1250
13075	97.500	: 0	500	0	5000	: 500	0	750	750
13175	97.000	: 500	0	0	4500	: 0	500	0	2000
20375	98.125	: 0	1125	0	5625	: 1125	0	625	875
20475	98.250	: 0	125	0	5750	: 125	0	0	1375
20575	98.250	: 0	0	0	5750	: 0	0	0	1375
20675	98.750	: 0	500	0	6250	: 500	0	625	875
20775	98.000	: 750	0	0	5500	: 0	750	0	2250
21075	99.250	: 0	1250	0	6750	: 1250	0	500	1000
21175	99.250	: 0	0	0	6750	: 0	0	0	1500
21275	99.000	: 250	0	0	6500	: 0	250	0	1750
21475	99.000	: 0	0	0	6500	: 0	0	0	1750
21875	98.750	: 250	0	0	6250	: 0	250	0	2000
21975	99.125	: 0	375	0	6625	: 375	0	0	1625
22075	99.000	: 125	0	0	6500	: 0	125	0	1750
22175	99.000	: 0	0	0	6500	: 0	0	0	1750
22475	99.000	: 0	0	0	6500	: 0	0	0	1750
22575	99.000	: 0	0	0	6500	: 0	0	0	1750
22675	98.375	: 625	0	0	5875	: 0	625	0	2375
22775	98.125	: 250	0	0	5625	: 0	250	0	2625
22875	98.000	: 125	0	0	5500	: 0	125	0	2750
30375	98.125	: 0	125	0	5625	: 125	0	0	2625
30475	99.125	: 0	0	0	5625	: 0	0	0	2625
30575	97.750	: 375	0	0	5250	: 0	375	0	3000
30675	98.125	: 0	375	0	5625	: 375	0	0	2625
30775	98.500	: 0	375	0	6000	: 375	0	0	2250
31075	98.375	: 125	0	0	5875	: 0	125	0	2375
31175	98.250	: 125	0	0	5750	: 0	125	0	2500
31275	98.000	: 250	0	0	5500	: 0	250	0	2750
31375	98.000	: 0	0	0	5500	: 0	0	0	2750
31475	98.000	: 0	0	0	5500	: 0	0	0	2750
31775	98.000	: 0	0	0	5500	: 0	0	0	2750
31875	98.000	: 0	0	0	5500	: 0	0	0	2750

Source: CBOT, Research Dept.

tion for the initial GNMA margin requirement. The complete data base covers a period from January to October 1975. During that time, the GNMA market gyrated from a yield of 8.59 percent to 7.99 percent and back to 9.09 percent.

The GNMA price movement simulation reveals the following facts:

1. If profits are not taken in a predetermined manner, the speculator will probably lose.
2. When yield levels are moving rapidly, daily price movements become more disorderly. The trading range increases.
3. Limit moves happen very rarely. Nevertheless, a trader must be financially prepared for their occurrence or risk being closed out.

With this knowledge, a trader of long-term Treasury bonds or GNMA contracts should be able to decide on a rational stop loss position that is suitable to a specific trading philosophy. Remember that a tight stop loss position exposes the trader to being whiplashed in and out of the market. This makes it difficult to generate net trading profits since commission charges become too large. Simultaneously, such a policy avoids significant losses. Understanding these trade-offs will certainly enable you to tailor a program to your specific trading objectives.

PLACING YOUR ORDER

Generally, orders are placed when a customer is ready to trade. If this action can be taken when a contract is opened or closed for the day, the execution of a commodity order probably will be more efficient. Since contracts are traded by open outcry, it is to the advantage of the customer to have many floor traders and scalpers in the pit when an order is executed. This usually occurs early in the morning or just before closing, since numerous traders add to and offset their own positions at these times. There are periods during the day when a trading pit contains only a few traders, making the competition at that moment for an entering order less than satisfactory.

Since neither you nor your broker normally can be aware of the number of floor traders present at any time, it is suggested that large orders be placed carefully.

SELECTING THE APPROPRIATE CONTRACT MONTH

A hedging strategy may often determine the contract selected for trading. However, when a choice is available, pay careful attention to pricing and contract liquidity. The latter can be obtained by your broker at any time and is also printed daily on the commodity pages of leading financial newspapers. If you contemplate trading 50 T-bill contracts and the September 1979 contract indicates an open position of 1,200 and the March 1980 contract an open position of 150, the September 1979 contract should be selected. If you must trade March 1980, select September 1979 now and roll the position forward at a later date. Despite the additional commission expense, the total result of the trade probably will be more satisfactory.

LIMITING MARGIN EXPOSURES

Do not permit your reach to exceed your grasp. If you have available a certain amount of dollars for speculative purposes, attempt to limit your initial margin requirements to 50 percent of your available balance. This will enable you to withstand momentary market setbacks without necessitating margin calls or the involuntary liquidation of a position. This rule may be the most difficult to follow, since it goes against the inherent grain of most speculators.

CROSS HEDGING

Be certain that you understand the risk associated with every transaction. Although numerous mathematical relationships can be developed between dissimilar securities, their price behavior may vary substantially during short periods of time. These variations must also be measured against the absolute price exposure of a security or money market instrument that is not cross hedged. If such risks are unacceptable, cross hedging should be avoided.

SELECTING YOUR PARTNER

A broker is a silent partner! In some ways, a registered commodity representative, often referred to as a RCR, is a limited partner. The analogy appears appropriate since the downside risk of the broker is limited to his or her intangible reputation, but the broker is guaranteed a profit in the form of commissions. Therefore, you should select your partner carefully. If you do not know a financially oriented representative, ask questions and carefully listen to the answers. The following queries make a good beginning:

1. What types of customers do you service? The question is meant to discern whether the broker handles speculative or hedge accounts. Ideally, both types of accounts should be managed, since a hedger may provide fundamental trade information to a broker.
2. What commodities do you trade? If the answer is all of them, hang up. Most RCRs specialize in one or two types of contracts. For instance, a representative specializing in grains may also be astute about meats, since the cost of feed is significant in computing the price of cattle. It would be most unusual for that individual also to have an in-depth knowledge of silver or orange juice.
3. How do you execute your orders? If possible, select a broker who has direct access to the trading floor for your commodity. Such an individual is generally able to execute your order more efficiently (at a better price) than a broker who writes a ticket that is simply transmitted to the wire house trading desk on the floor of an exchange. Direct access is hard to find but worth pursuing.
4. What is your prior business experience? If you are interested in trading interest rate futures, it would make sense to locate someone with an economics background or business experience in a financial capacity. It generally helps to understand a script if you have read it before!

Since it is probably impossible to identify someone with all of these attributes, select a broker who has one or two of these characteristics and with whom you feel comfortable. Equally important, make certain that your business is significant to the broker. Unlike trading stocks, you must offset your futures trade with the same firm that processed your initial position. Therefore, it is impractical to buy from one and sell through another broker or dealer. Do your homework before you leap!

Appendix

Normal trading practice among dealers and in the Federal Reserve's weekly auction requires all bids to be based on the bank discount rate which is also the T-bill yield—the phrases are used interchangeably. But, because the bank discount rate is calculated in a unique fashion, a person attempting to equate T-bill yields with bond yields must convert the T-bill rate to a bond equivalent rate.

Essentially, the bank discount rate is the difference between the face value of a bill and its market value on an annualized basis. Formulas for determining price, T-bill yield (bank discount rate), and equivalent bond yield follow:

1. To determine the T-bill actual issue price:

$$\$1,000,000 - \frac{(\text{Days to maturity} \times \text{T-bill yield} \times \$1,000,000)}{360} = \text{Actual issue price}$$

Example: Given, 6% T-bill yield on a 91-day bill

$$\$1,000,000 - \frac{(91 \times 0.06 \times \$1,000,000)}{360} = \$984,833.33 \ (\text{issue price})$$

2. To determine the T-bill yield when T-bill face value, days to maturity, and actual issue price are known:

$$\frac{\dfrac{(\text{T-bill face value} - \text{Actual issue price}) \times 360}{\text{Days to maturity}}}{\text{T-bill face value}} = \text{T-bill yield}$$

Example: Given, \$1,000,000, 91-day T-bill with actual issue price of \$984,833.33

$$\frac{\dfrac{(\$1,000,000 - \$984,833.33) \times 360}{91}}{\$1,000,000} = 6.00\% \ \text{T-bill yield}$$

3. T-bill yield to equivalent bond yield

$$\frac{\dfrac{(\text{T-bill face value} - \text{Actual issue price}) \times 365}{\text{Days to maturity}}}{\text{Actual issue price}} = \text{Equivalent bond yield}$$

Example:

$$\frac{\dfrac{(\$1,000,000 - \$984,833.33) \times 365}{91}}{\$984,833.33} = 6.18\% \ \text{equivalent bond yield}$$

Source: Chicago Mercantile Exchange, Treasury Bill Futures, p. 27.

Exhibit B
Payment schedule for a $25,000, 9 percent direct reduction
FHA loan with a 30-year maturity
(payments 1-60 and 301-360)

PAY'T NO.	INTEREST PAYMENT	PRINCIPAL PAYMENT	BALANCE OF LOAN	PAY'T NO.	INTEREST PAYMENT	PRINCIPAL PAYMENT	BALANCE OF LOAN
1	187.50	13.66	24,986.34	301	72.64	128.52	9,556.80
2	187.40	13.76	24,972.58	302	71.68	129.48	9,427.32
3	187.29	13.87	24,958.71	303	70.70	130.46	9,296.86
4	187.19	13.97	24,944.74	304	69.73	131.43	9,165.43
5	187.09	14.07	24,930.67	305	68.74	132.42	9,033.01
6	186.98	14.18	24,916.49	306	67.75	133.41	8,899.60
7	186.87	14.29	24,902.20	307	66.75	134.41	8,765.19
8	186.77	14.39	24,887.81	308	65.74	135.42	8,629.77
9	186.66	14.50	24,873.31	309	64.72	136.44	8,493.33
10	186.55	14.61	24,858.70	310	63.70	137.46	8,355.87
11	186.44	14.72	24,843.98	311	62.67	138.49	8,217.38
12	186.33	14.83	24,829.15	312	61.63	139.53	8,077.85
13	186.22	14.94	24,814.21	313	60.58	140.58	7,937.27
14	186.11	15.05	24,799.16	314	59.53	141.63	7,795.64
15	185.99	15.17	24,783.99	315	58.47	142.69	7,652.95
16	185.88	15.28	24,768.71	316	57.40	143.76	7,509.19
17	185.77	15.39	24,753.32	317	56.32	144.84	7,364.35
18	185.65	15.51	24,737.81	318	55.23	145.93	7,218.42
19	185.53	15.63	24,722.18	319	54.14	147.02	7,071.40
20	185.42	15.74	24,706.44	320	53.04	148.12	6,923.28
21	185.30	15.86	24,690.58	321	51.92	149.24	6,774.04
22	185.18	15.98	24,674.60	322	50.81	150.35	6,623.69
23	185.06	16.10	24,658.50	323	49.68	151.48	6,472.21
24	184.94	16.22	24,642.28	324	48.54	152.62	6,319.59
25	184.82	16.34	24,625.94	325	47.40	153.76	6,165.83
26	184.69	16.47	24,609.47	326	46.24	154.92	6,010.91
27	184.57	16.59	24,592.88	327	45.08	156.08	5,854.83
28	184.45	16.71	24,576.17	328	43.91	157.25	5,697.58
29	184.32	16.84	24,559.33	329	42.73	158.43	5,539.15
30	184.19	16.97	24,542.36	330	41.54	159.62	5,379.53
31	184.07	17.09	24,525.27	331	40.35	160.81	5,218.72
32	183.94	17.22	24,508.05	332	39.14	162.02	5,056.70
33	183.81	17.35	24,490.70	333	37.93	163.23	4,893.47
34	183.68	17.48	24,473.22	334	36.70	164.46	4,729.01
35	183.55	17.61	24,455.61	335	35.47	165.69	4,563.32
36	183.42	17.74	24,437.87	336	34.22	166.94	4,396.38
37	183.28	17.88	24,419.99	337	32.97	168.19	4,228.19
38	183.15	18.01	24,401.98	338	31.71	169.45	4,058.74
39	183.01	18.15	24,383.83	339	30.44	170.72	3,888.02
40	182.88	18.28	24,365.55	340	29.16	172.00	3,716.02
41	182.74	18.42	24,347.13	341	27.87	173.29	3,542.73
42	182.60	18.56	24,328.57	342	26.57	174.59	3,368.14
43	182.46	18.70	24,309.87	343	25.26	175.90	3,192.24
44	182.32	18.84	24,291.03	344	23.94	177.22	3,015.02
45	182.18	18.98	24,272.05	345	22.61	178.55	2,836.47
46	182.04	19.12	24,252.93	346	21.27	179.89	2,656.58
47	181.90	19.26	24,233.67	347	19.92	181.24	2,475.34
48	181.75	19.41	24,214.26	348	18.57	182.59	2,292.75
49	181.61	19.55	24,194.71	349	17.20	183.96	2,108.79
50	181.46	19.70	24,175.01	350	15.82	185.34	1,923.45
51	181.31	19.85	24,155.16	351	14.43	186.73	1,736.72
52	181.16	20.00	24,135.16	352	13.03	188.13	1,548.59
53	181.01	20.15	24,115.01	353	11.61	189.55	1,359.04
54	180.86	20.30	24,094.71	354	10.19	190.97	1,168.07
55	180.71	20.45	24,074.26	355	8.76	192.40	975.67
56	180.56	20.60	24,053.66	356	7.32	193.84	781.83
57	180.40	20.76	24,032.90	357	5.86	195.30	586.53
58	180.25	20.91	24,011.99	358	4.40	196.76	389.77
59	180.09	21.07	23,990.92	359	2.92	198.24	191.53
60	179.93	21.23	23,969.69	360	1.44	191.53	.00

FINAL PAYMENT: 192.97

Source: Boston: Financial Publishing Co.

204

Exhibit C
Collateralized depository receipt

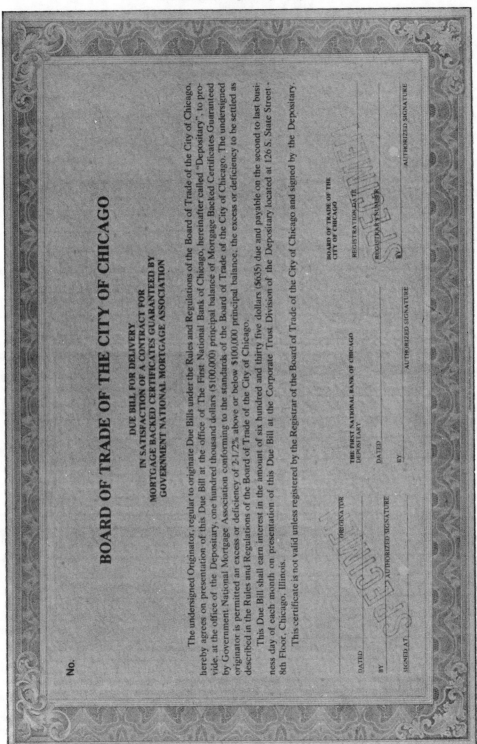

© 1978, Chicago Board of Trade.

Exhibit D
Trade confirmation

Exhibit E
Purchase and sale report

740-000011 095
ACCOUNT NO.

DEAN WITTER REYNOLDS INC.
2 BROADWAY, NEW YORK, N. Y. 10004

05-12-78 PAGE
DATE

COMMODITY DIVISION

STATEMENT OF PURCHASES
AND/OR SALES

CONFIRMATION OF THESE COMPLETED
TRANSACTIONS HAS BEEN SENT TO
YOU UNDER SEPARATE COVER.

TYPE OF ACCOUNT
4. REGULATED COMMODITY
5. UNREG. COMMODITY

*SEE REVERSE SIDE FOR ADDITIONAL CONDITIONS

TRADE DATE	QUANTITY BOUGHT	QUANTITY SOLD	DESCRIPTION	MKT	TYPE	PRICE OR EXPLANATION	DIFFERENCE	FEE	COMMISSION	NET AMOUNT TO YOUR ACCOUNT
04 27 78	1		DEC 78 GNMA	A	4	92 2/32				
05 05 78		1	DEC 78 GNMA	A	4	91 30/32	125.00	1.00	75.00	49.00 PROFIT
			1 GNMA			P&S 381				
			** FINAL TOTAL **				125.00	1.00	75.00	49.00 PROFIT

Exhibit F

Customer monthly statement

PAGE 1

STATEMENT DATE 06/30/76

DEAN WITTER REYNOLDS INC.

2 BROADWAY   NEW YORK, N.Y. 10004

ACCOUNT NUMBER 1

TYPE OF ACCOUNT
4-REGULATED COMMODITY   5-UNREGULATED COMMODITY
G CASH OR SPOT COMMODITY

740-000011-5-049

YOUR ACCOUNTS ARE LISTED BELOW, EACH TYPE
OF ACCOUNT IS INDICATED IN THIS COLUMN

DATE	BOUGHT RECEIVED OR LONG	SOLD DELIVERED OR SHORT	DESCRIPTION	PRICE OR EXPLANATION*	DEBIT	CREDIT	BALANCE DEBIT UNLESS MARKED CR	TYPE
6/08	1		SEP 76 GNMA	91 4/32				4
6/08	1		SEP 76 GNMA	91				4
			BALANCE FWD 05/31/76				3,745.00CR	4
			CLOSING BALANCE				3,745.00CR	4
			MONTH-TO-DATE PROFIT/LOSS				0.00	
			YEAR-TO-DATE PROFIT/LOSS				384.25	
			OPEN CONTRACTS					
6/08	1		SEP 76 GNMA	91 5/32				4
6/08	1		SEP 76 GNMA	91				4
6/30	2		SETTLE PRICE	89 31/32	UNREALIZED LOSS		2,343.75	4
					NET UNREALIZED LOSS		2,343.75	4
					NET EQUITY		1,405.25CR	4
							COMPLETE	

E. & O. E.

IF THIS STATEMENT IS NOT IN ACCORDANCE WITH YOUR RECORDS, PLEASE
INFORM YOUR ACCOUNT EXECUTIVE OR THE OFFICE SERVICING YOUR ACCOUNT.

* SEE REVERSE SIDE

Exhibit G
Margin notice

DEAN WITTER REYNOLDS INC.
2 Broadway, New York, NY 10004

Date: 78-06-21

Dear Client:

As you have previously been advised, commodity margin calls are due on demand. Therefore, **TOTAL FUNDS DUE** must be paid in full within two (2) business days from the date of this notice.
Your cooperation in satisfying this obligation is appreciated and will avoid the necessity of our having to liquidate your account to satisfy existing House or Exchange requirements.

Your original requirement was . . . . $.00

Your maintenance restoration requirement is . . $845.00

Any previously outstanding calls are . . . . . $.00

TOTAL FUNDS DUE are $845.00

If you have already remitted the funds called for herein, please disregard this notice. If only a partial payment has been made, please send the balance due us along with the stub below to the office servicing your account.

THANK YOU _____
Commodity Margin Clerk

Account
Number 740 000011 = 044

PLEASE DETACH AND RETURN THIS STUB WITH YOUR CHECK TO THE OFFICE SERVICING YOUR ACCOUNT

Index

Buy limit order, 24
Buy stop limit order, 25
Buy stop order, 24-25

C

Call for money, 13
Cash commodity, 27
Cash forward market, 27
Cash market
  commodity trading distinguished, 5-7
  interest rate futures distinguished, 93-94
Certificate delivery contract, 55
Charting concepts, 83-92
  bar chart, 84-89
  moving-average charts, 90
  point-and-figure chart, 90-92
  tools, 84
  value, 92
Chartists, 83
  basic philosophy behind, 83
Cheap, 28
Chicago Board of Trade (CBOT), vii, 12
  advantage of, 12
  commercial paper contract traded on, 21
  direct-delivery GNMA contract traded on, 21
  formation, 2
  GNMA certificate delivery; see GNMA certificate delivery
  GNMA mortgage interest rate contract traded, 21
  memberships in, 22
  number of members, 22
  purposes, 2
  Treasury bond traded on, 21
Chicago Mercantile Exchange (Merc), 2
  number of members, 22
  Treasury bill contract traded on, 21
Clearing corporation
  defined, 13
  establishment of, 12-13
  responsibilities of, 13
Clearing Corporation of the Board of Trade of the City of Chicago
  formation, 2
  function, 2
Clearinghouse, 2, 28
Collateralized depository receipts (CDRs), 21, 28, 32-33, 55, 205
  adjustment of traders' trading accounts, 105-6
  calculation of equivalent principal balances, 56-58, 103
  conversion factor, 57-58, 103
  defined, 102

Collateralized depository receipts—*Cont.*
  delivery of, 104-5
  delivery day, 104-5
  delivery rules, 101-9
  endorsement of, 104
  intention day, 104-5
  Notice of Intention to Deliver, 104-5
  origination of, 101-3, 109
  originator's duties after origination of, 106-7
  pricing, 55-58
  registration, 104-5
  surrender of, 107-9
Commercial bank regulations, 160-61
Commercial paper loan futures contracts, 21, 38
  adjustment of traders' trading accounts, 123-25
  contract grade, 120
  delivery rules, 119-25
  financial receipts
    creation of, 120-22
    defined, 120
    delivery of, 119-20, 122-23
    endorsement of, 122
    registration, 122-23
    surrender, 125
    transfer, 121-22
  important general features, 119-20
  long hedge by issuer, 134
  pricing fundamentals, 69, 71
  trading process, 133-35
  vault for safekeeping, 120-21
Commodity exchange
  daily trading volume, 22-23
  day trader, 23-24
  defined, 22
  floor broker, 23
  floor traders, 23-24
  governing of, 22
  interest rate futures contracts traded on, 21
  limit order, 24, 26
  market order, 24
  memberships in, 22
  money pits, 22
  order-processing cycle, 25-26
  orders frequently processed, 24-25; see also specific orders
  scalpers, 23-24
  special memberships, 22
  speculator, 23
  stop limit order, 25
  stop orders, 24-25
  trading on, 21-38
Commodity Exchange Act of 1936, 4
Commodity Exchange Authority, 4

212